What people are saying about …

A Student's Guide to Culture

"Here's an invaluable resource for understanding our culture—but equally important, how each of us can play a role in influencing it for Christ. There are keen insights, profound wisdom, and godly vision in these pages. Keep a highlighter handy—you'll need it!"

Lee Strobel, bestselling author of *The Case for Christ* and *The Case for Faith*

"Better than anything I've read, this book puts the immoral issues you're curious and concerned about in the big-picture context of our chaotic culture. With every chapter you read, you'll understand more about why this matters. You will believe you were 'created for such a time as this' as you read. And you'll know what to do with the passion that bubbles up within you because of the practical action steps and many truths in these pages."

Kathy Koch, PhD, founder and president of Celebrate Kids, Inc.

"I am thrilled to see this practical and yet timely book to help students navigate the toughest issues today with biblical wisdom. This is an indispensable guide for any young person who wants to know how to think and live Christianly in this generation."

Sean McDowell, PhD, professor, speaker, author

"*A Student's Guide to Culture* is the most important book your young Christians will read this year. It's packed with biblical truth and insight on topics young believers contemplate on a daily basis. John Stonestreet and Brett Kunkle address the most critical issues of culture, helping students to understand *why* they should care, *what* they are facing, and *how* they can navigate the culture in a way that honors God and reflects a Christian worldview. If you're a parent, pastor, or youth volunteer, get this book for your students."

J. Warner Wallace, cold-case detective, adjunct professor, author, and creator of the Case Makers Academy for Kids

"John Stonestreet and Brett Kunkle have created one of the most practical and insightful resources in helping this generation think Christianly amidst the chaos and undercurrent of a confusing culture. In one work, they have answered *the why* and *the how* to understanding and engaging culture through the grid of Scripture. I believe *A Student's Guide to Culture* is a needed breath of fresh air, and I can't wait to see its impact in churches, schools, and families."

Brent Crowe, PhD, vice president of Student Leadership University, slulead.com

"How can you navigate today's post-Christian culture without being shaped by it? How do you maintain hope in a culture of outrage? In *A Student's Guide to Culture*, Brett Kunkle and John Stonestreet will skillfully guide you as you learn how to think clearly and carefully about your faith and then talk about it with others who don't share your Christian convictions. In this practical book, you will learn how to withstand the challenging waves of culture and make a lasting difference."

Jonathan Morrow, author of *Welcome to College* and creator of 5 Things Every Teenager Needs to Build a Lasting Faith

"If there was ever a time in history when students needed a practical guide to help them navigate the ideas that shape their culture it's now. And no one is better equipped to prepare them than Brett Kunkle and John Stonestreet. *A Student's Guide to Culture* is an important resource to help our kids live out a vibrant faith in a post-Christian world."

Alisa Childers, author, speaker, and
former CCM recording artist

A
Student's Guide
to Culture

John Stonestreet & Brett Kunkle

A
Student's Guide
to Culture

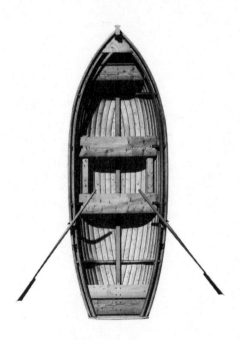

DAVID C COOK

transforming lives together

A STUDENT'S GUIDE TO CULTURE
Published by David C Cook
4050 Lee Vance Drive
Colorado Springs, CO 80918 U.S.A.

Integrity Music Limited, a Division of David C Cook
Brighton, East Sussex BN1 2RE, England

The graphic circle C logo is a registered trademark of David C Cook.

The website addresses recommended throughout this book are offered as a
resource to you. These websites are not intended in any way to be or imply an
endorsement on the part of David C Cook, nor do we vouch for their content.

Unless otherwise noted, all Scripture quotations are taken from the ESV® Bible
(The Holy Bible, English Standard Version®), copyright © 2001 by Crossway, a
publishing ministry of Good News Publishers. Used by permission. All rights
reserved. Scripture quotations marked THE MESSAGE are taken from THE MESSAGE.
Copyright © by Eugene H. Peterson 1993, 2002. Used by permission of Tyndale
House Publishers, Inc.; and NASB are taken from the New American Standard Bible®,
copyright © 1960, 1995 by The Lockman Foundation. Used by permission. (www.
Lockman.org). The authors have added italics to Scripture quotations for emphasis.

Library of Congress Control Number 2019948089
ISBN 978-0-8307-7877-5
eISBN 978-0-8307-7878-2

© 2020 John Stonestreet and Brett Kunkle
Content adapted from *A Practical Guide to Culture* © 2017 John Stonestreet
and Brett Kunkle. Published by David C Cook, ISBN 978-1-4347-1101-4.

The Team: Stephanie Bennett, Toben Heim,
Amy Konyndyk, Jack Campbell, Susan Murdock
Cover Design: Nick Lee
Cover Photo: Getty Images

Printed in the United States of America
First Edition 2020

1 2 3 4 5 6 7 8 9 10

101519

for Lexi, Micah, Paige, Ella, and Jonah
and
for Abigail, Anna, Alison, and Hunter

Discussion questions for each chapter are available
for your youth ministry or small group.

To request your free digital copy of
the questions, contact David C Cook
at customercare@davidccook.org
or 800-323-7543.

Contents

Part Four: Building a Christian Worldview

Introduction

I (Brett) love surfing. I grew up in Southern California, started surfing in junior high, and have been at it ever since. My coauthor, John, not so much. He's landlocked in Colorado. After years of riding waves, I can tell you there are few things like it. Riding a wave is an amazing experience.

However, the ocean can also be a punishing place. I've ridden waves but been pounded by them too. Waves have held me underwater long enough for panic to set in as I felt myself run out of oxygen. I've wiped out plenty of times. A few years ago, after a big fall on a big wave, I even herniated discs in my lower back. And I've seen people get in serious trouble in the rip currents. One time, after pulling an unconscious boy from the deep waters of the ocean, I watched a lifeguard perform CPR and save the boy's life. I love the ocean, but I know it's a dangerous place.

Just like there are amazing, gorgeous beaches and oceans around the world, there are so many beautiful parts of culture. Wonderful people. Awe-inspiring art. Amazing technology. Massive cities. However, some parts of culture will pound you. False ideas. Harmful practices and customs. Even life-destroying habits.

You've probably seen the harm firsthand. Maybe a close friend has been pounded by the cultural waves, drowning in substance abuse, casual sex, or addiction to technology. Maybe you've seen relationships broken by social media. Or maybe you've taken a beating by the culture, and now you find yourself swimming in a sea of anxiety and depression. Life in our culture can be rough. And if John and I are going to be completely honest, we don't think it will get better anytime soon. The cultural currents are getting stronger, and the cultural waves are pounding harder.

So, as a follower of Jesus Christ, here's the big question: How do you keep from drowning? How do you live in culture but not be taken captive by it? How can you be "in the world" but not "of it"?

The church needs a new generation of Christians who can keep their heads above water and navigate the challenges of today's world. However, we're not talking about narrowly surviving. That's not enough. Just like a surfer can take a beating by big waves and barely make it back to shore, the culture can pound your faith and leave you with no desire to paddle back out into the waves. But for followers of Jesus, giving up is not an option. No, we actually have Good News for the culture. The Gospel of Jesus not only rescues us from our sin, it shows us a better way to be human in this broken and sinful world and gives us a new path to follow—one that leads to thriving and flourishing, no matter what else is happening around us. In Jesus, we *always* have hope. And Jesus tells us to take that hope back into the culture.

That's the purpose of this book. We want to help you navigate today's culture successfully *and* then go back into the world with love, truth, and courage as you proclaim the hope found only in Christ.

Now, before you dive in, it will help you to understand how this book is organized and why it is structured that way. You might be tempted to jump right into the hot topics. Porn. Hooking up. Sexual orientation. Gender identity. Racism. Atheism. Whatever. And of course, we need to think carefully about every one of those issues.

However, that approach won't be as helpful. Why? Because each of these smaller, isolated issues fits into a much bigger picture. Just like a single paragraph in a full-length book won't make much sense apart from the larger story, God's thoughts on an individual topic won't make as much sense without understanding His larger story of the world. So, you'll need to patiently and thoughtfully work your way through parts 1 and 2 because the knowledge you'll gain in those chapters will help you make sense of the specific topics we'll cover in part 3. Lastly, just like a surfer needs the right equipment—a good wet suit, a custom-shaped board, sunscreen—you'll need some good tools too, and that's what we'll give you in part 4.

Are you ready to begin? You have to study, train, and practice before you paddle out into the ocean to ride serious waves. Likewise, preparation will get you ready to paddle out into the culture, and reading this book is an essential step in your training.

Let's go.

Part One

Why You Should Care about Culture

Chapter One

What Culture Is and How It Shapes Us

"If you want to know what water is, don't ask the fish."
Ancient Chinese Proverb

Fish don't know they're wet.

In one sense, of course, there is nothing fish know more than water. They spend their entire lives in it. But the proverb above highlights how hard it is to know, understand, and evaluate the environment we're in all the time. It can even be difficult to realize that we're in an environment, which makes it impossible to resist the surrounding conditions. What we're immersed in *just* becomes the norm.

Culture is to humans what water is to fish—the environment where we live and move and eat and work and play and, therefore, think is normal. But there's a big difference between us and fish—we create our own environment; fish don't. Think about it. Human beings impose themselves on the world in a way that animals don't and can't. Animals take the world as it is and then live in that world. They eat, sleep, and reproduce. That's about it. Fish or dolphins or wolves or lions aren't getting together to create cultures or entire civilizations. That's utterly unique to human beings. We take the world and then form our own new little worlds out of the larger world. Our ability to create culture makes us vastly different from animals.

But like fish in water, we can become so immersed in our ways of thinking and patterns of living that we develop blind spots and lose sight of how culture shapes us. We lose our ability to see problems and find it hard to resist the temptation to do what everyone else is doing.

Think of being unaware of the sheer beauty of a mountain you've always lived near or not recognizing the dysfunction of an abusive family because it's the only kind you've ever known. In the same way, culture shapes our perception of reality in ways we don't always recognize.

If we don't do the hard, intentional work of examining the world around us, it won't occur to us that things should be any different. Few things shape us like the ideas, customs, habits, and influences of culture. So it's vital we become fully aware of the cultural forces impacting our lives.

Of course, as Christians, our truest identity is determined by God. Scripture tells us we are the pinnacle of God's creation. We bear His image (Gen. 1:26–28). As such, we're much more than mere products of culture.

This is critical because how a culture views and values human life plays a huge role in whether it's healthy or not. Of all the reasons to be *intentional* to make sense of culture, this is the most important. We must never lose sight of the biblical vision of who we are as the most precious of God's creation.

You may be tempted to think, *When are we going to get to the really interesting stuff? Enough of all this theory and culture talk. I need help navigating issues like gender identity and transitioning, Snapchat, white privilege or #BlackLivesMatter, being gay and evolution. Let's skip to the practical stuff.*

We get it. Those issues are front and center in our culture. You face them almost every single day. But if you can be patient and trust us, we'll get there. Understanding the goal of this book may help you keep pushing through. We're not interested in merely talking about and analyzing culture. We want to help you *live well* in the culture. To be human and to be alive means we have to live in culture, deal with all this "stuff," and navigate the cultural land mines of ideas, values, issues, and structures. So, thinking well *and* living well are our goals.

But it's a daunting task. The hot topics may be obvious, but there are a bunch of cultural undercurrents that shape how we think and live. Beneath the "waves" that dominate news headlines and social-media feeds are the subtle, yet important, cultural "undercurrents." Sadly, a lot of Christians are oblivious to these unseen issues and, therefore, have no way of resisting their negative impact.

You must first understand these undercurrents in order to fully grasp the specific issues discussed later in the book. After all, the most powerful way culture shapes and influences us is in what it presents as being *normal*. For example, before you got your first smartphone (for the 95 percent of you who have one!), did you spend any time asking questions like, *Should I even own a smartphone? How will a smartphone shape my heart and mind? Can a smartphone actually harm me in serious ways?* Those questions never cross the minds of most people. Why? Because in our culture, owning a smartphone is just so normal. We make sure we own one because it would be abnormal *not to*.

But clearly, not everything accepted as normal *ought* to be, right? And that's why we can't just dive straight into the hot cultural topics. We need to look beneath the surface of culture. As Christian thinker C. S. Lewis said, "The most dangerous ideas in a society are not the ones that are being argued, but the ones that are assumed."[1]

Back to the smartphone question. Is it wrong to own one? Of course not. We own them. However, we have also done a lot of careful thinking about how smartphones shape our lives and relationships. Studies show a risk for addiction and links between smartphone use and anxiety and depression. Yes, too much time on that device will impact your mental health. Despite how normal smartphones are, they're not harmless.

This is an example of a cultural undercurrent, something going on beneath the surface that most people aren't aware of. It's a cultural blind spot, and every culture has them. Thinking they don't exist reveals our ignorance not only of the subtle power culture has over our hearts and minds but also of the universal fallen human condition that infects all people in all times and all places.

So, don't make the mistake of jumping right into the hot topics. For the sake of your own future, you should think clearly about the most important issues of our time *as well as* the dehumanizing undercurrents driving those issues. That's why we're going to spend some time thinking carefully about culture itself.

To start, let's get clear on what culture *is* and what it *is not*. An accurate definition of *culture* will help you see how it shapes you and what it is made of.

What Culture Is (and What It Is Not)

Culture is a much-used word that's rarely defined.[2] It comes from the Latin word *cultura*, which means "agriculture." If plowing, tilling, and cultivating come to mind, they should. In its most basic sense, culture refers to what people do with their world: we build, we invent, we imagine, we create, we tear down, we replace, we compose, we design, we emphasize, we dismiss, we embellish, we engineer.

As author Andy Crouch says, "Culture is what human beings make of the world."[3] It's not what we do by instinct, like circulating blood, eating food, or sleeping. It's more what we do freely, like donating blood for a good cause, topping pizza with canned tuna (popular in Germany), or taking a nap in the afternoon (what Spaniards call a *siesta*).

Cultivating is exactly the sort of behavior we should expect from human beings made in God's image. After all, God's first command to Adam and Eve, and thus to all humanity, was to "be fruitful and multiply and fill the earth and subdue it" (Gen. 1:28). God made humans with the capacity to do something with His world, and that's exactly what we do. It was part of God's plan from the beginning.

Another term found within the word *culture* can add to our understanding. It's the word *cult*. To be clear, we're *not* talking about a commune where people share all their possessions and chant together ten times a day. In this case the word *cult* points to the deeply held religious beliefs of a culture. We all have ideas about God, truth, morality, humanity, and the purpose of life. Those beliefs form our *worldview*. And our worldview, regardless if we're consciously aware of it, shapes our actions and our inter-actions with others.

All of us have "belief glasses," or a worldview through which we see the world. We don't look *at* our worldview; we look *through* it. It's the story through which we see and make sense of the real world.

The cultures we create reflect our worldview commitments. This is why cultures differ so greatly from one time and place to another. As Christian apologist Ravi Zacharias says, "In some cultures, people love their neighbors. In other cultures, they eat them." Differences between cultures reveal dramatic differences of worldview. Shifts within a culture, like those that have taken place over the past few decades in the United States, reveal deeper shifts in our worldview.

Two more insights will help us understand culture and its power to shape us. First, *culture isn't fixed or static*. It's dynamic. Culture changes with human innovations, inventions, and ideas. Not all generations are equally comfortable with the way a culture changes. That's why your grandma may shake her head at your latest pair of ripped jeans, the newest Netflix series you and all your friends are bingeing, and other lifestyle choices you make, and vice versa.

Second, *culture includes smaller subcultures*. Though some cultural norms span entire sections of people within a country or society (like high-ways, internet access, and the federal government), there are other things (like trends, fashions, and ways of life) that distinguish groups of people from others within the same larger culture. For instance, the hairstyles, clothing, and music popular in Southern California may be really different from those in the Pacific Northwest or the Deep South. There can even be different subcultures on the same school campus, from the athletes to the brains to the emos and goths to the populars. Especially in a massive coun-try like the United States, it's more accurate to speak of cultures (plural) than of the culture (singular). Subcultures also have tremendous power to influence our thoughts and actions.

How Culture Shapes Us

Humans externalize their values, imaginations, innovations, and ideas onto the world around them by what they say and do. Basically, we take what's going on inside of us (in our hearts and minds) and we put it on the outside for all to see. A producer makes a movie, a fashion designer creates a clothing line, and an author writes a book—all examples of externalization.

Cultural norms are powerful. They determine much of our daily lives: our schedules, what we like and don't like, what we eat, what we wear, and how we spend our money. We settle into our culture's routines, lifestyles, and habits. For example, what you see your friends or celebrities or athletes "externalizing" on their Instagram feeds can influence you to buy a certain product, wear certain brands, or adopt certain values. As we consume our culture's products, ideas, and assumptions about the world, it shapes our lives by defining what is normal.

We can summarize these concepts with our analogy from the book's introduction: culture is like an ocean. When you swim in the ocean, you get wet. Splash around a bit and you'll get the people around you wet too. In the same way, we're all swimming (living) in the waters of culture and we're splashing it—the ideas and values—onto one another every single day. The difference is, you can't get out of this ocean. We live in it 24/7.

And that's the danger.

If you're not careful, you will find yourself becoming culture shaped rather than a culture shaper.

What Culture Is Made Of

So, what's in the water? What is culture made of? There are four important categories in culture you should be able to recognize.

First, culture is made up of *ideas*. In a diverse society like ours, there are many different ideas about life and the world. For example, many people think that truth, goodness, and beauty are mere matters of opinion—that is, subjective—rather than objective facts about the world. That's why you hear people make statements like, "You do you. I'll do me." They've been influenced by ideas in the culture. As members of society, when such ideas are presented to us as the norm, we often absorb them.

Second, ideas spread in a culture through *champions*. Certainly, this includes schoolteachers, college professors, and other academic types. However, originators of ideas rarely change culture without significant help from artists, storytellers, entrepreneurs, celebrities, and influencers who communicate their ideas through a third aspect, *artifacts*. An artifact can be a song, book, movie, class, podcast, invention, or social-media feed. The Protestant Reformation in the 1500s shifted culture in profound ways. But without the invention of the printing press that helped spike literacy rates by making books, especially the Bible, more accessible to everyday people, it wouldn't have.

Fourth, *institutions* maintain culture. An institution is a collection of people trying to accomplish a similar purpose. The most important institutions of a society are the family, church, and government. However, there is an endless list of other cultural institutions, such as sports teams, athletic leagues, schools, universities, clubs, businesses, media, and so on. And what determines how these institutions operate? Culture.

In our culture, educational institutions like schools and universities are viewed as the experts on knowledge. What's true and right and good is whatever is taught in schools and universities. In the United States, the media decides what counts as news. When media outlets spend most of their time on the latest celebrity gossip while ignoring disturbing videos about the abortion industry or the persecution of Christians, they're telling us what news and issues are most important.

When social institutions change, so does culture. Since the 1970s, shifts in the family, such as no-fault divorce, living together before marriage, and extended singleness, have significantly reshaped American culture. As the church becomes less important in the everyday lives of citizens, other sources of moral authority become more important—and not for the better.

The Lord Jesus calls Christians not to be "conformed to this world, but ... transformed by the renewal of [our minds]" (Rom. 12:2). Resisting the cultural tidal wave may, at first, seem impossible. Thankfully, God's given us a Story bigger than the current cultural moment that makes it possible.

Chapter Two

Don't Confuse the Moment and the Story

"No, the Bible isn't a book of rules, or a book of heroes. The Bible is most of all a Story ... [and] the best thing about this Story is—it's true."
Sally Lloyd-Jones, *The Jesus Storybook Bible*

Throughout history, most Christians have found themselves in antagonistic cultures. For example, early Christians in the Roman Empire often faced terrible persecution. Followers of Christ lost their lives in a number of horrific ways, including being crucified, lit on fire, or thrown to hungry lions for sport. But that didn't stop many Christians from living out their faith.

During that time, children, unborn and born, were considered disposable. Abortion was common. Other babies were killed through a practice called *exposure*. Roman families who didn't wish to feed additional mouths would abandon newborns in the wild to die. Though exposure was legally and culturally acceptable at the time, Christians quickly embraced a different practice. They rescued these children, adopted them into their families, and raised them in the church.

Their actions were redemptive and praiseworthy, but there's more to the story.

Because newborn girls were the most common victims of exposure, within a couple of decades a gender imbalance developed in many Roman towns. When Roman men wanted to find wives, it was Christian families who had a great number of eligible young women. Many Roman men converted to Christianity in order to marry. According to sociologist Rodney Stark, this is among the factors that explain the explosive growth of Christianity in the second century.[1]

In the midst of a culture of death, Christians brought life, hope, and redemption, both physically and spiritually.

The Story and the Moment

God is always at work through—and at times even *in spite of*—His people. He is at work today as well. Everywhere, for those with eyes to see, is evidence of that work. God is using His people to lead nations out of poverty, create brilliant art, tell life-changing stories, adopt orphans, heal the sick, and restore broken lives and cultures.[2]

As Christians, we belong to a larger Story that God has been writing since before the beginning of time. When we allow ourselves to be shaped by His Story, we'll be better equipped to make a difference in our cultural moment. This is why Scripture is absolutely essential for followers of Jesus.

Christians contend the Bible is true. It's not just true *for us* or one truth among many truths, rather the Scriptures are *objectively* true. In other words, the Scriptures describe reality as it actually is.

Obviously, many people do not share this view of the Bible. But their unbelief doesn't change the truth. If you refuse to believe in gravity, will that stop you from falling if you jump out of a two-story building? Of course not. In the same way, the Scriptures are true whether we believe them or not.

The Bible is not merely a collection of nice stories or moral lessons. It doesn't just tell us how to be "spiritual." The Bible describes the Big Story of reality. Notice it doesn't start "once upon a time," but "in the beginning." It provides the overarching Story of the world, humanity, and history. God's Word tells us where everything came from, including us, and where everything is going, including us.

This point is crucial to rightly understand and approach culture: No matter how chaotic, grave, disturbing, broken, or troubling our cultural moment may be, its full meaning is revealed only in light of the larger Story of which it is a part. We must learn to approach our cultural moment from the Big Story; otherwise, we'll miss the meaning of both the moment and the Story.

Imagine someone abandoning The Lord of the Rings trilogy because he was angry that [Spoiler alert for this and the next two paragraphs!] Gandalf fell off the bridge as he was fighting the demon-like Balrog near the end of the first book.

"What kind of author kills off such a cool character as Gandalf?" he complains. "I want nothing to do with that kind of story!"

Anyone who's seen The Lord of the Rings movies or read the books would protest, "Wait! That's not the whole story. Gandalf doesn't die. He comes back. And he's no longer Gandalf the Grey; he's Gandalf the White. And in the end, he's part of the good that defeats evil."

Like our fictional Lord of the Rings reader, we're also at risk of losing the Story in the heat of the cultural moment, particularly when the world seems to be spinning out of control. Reeling from a tragic school shooting or political scandal, overwhelmed by porn addiction, trying to navigate a world where wrong is right and sin is popular, Christians often become reactionary and approach culture by asking the wrong question first.

"Where Should I Draw the Line?"

Christians often divide the world into sacred and secular, or spiritual and worldly. Everything on the spiritual side is good. Everything on the worldly side is bad. So when they approach culture, their primary concern is to keep from crossing the line from good to bad.

We draw lines like this all the time: all Christian music is good and all secular music is bad. Rated R movies are off limits, so Christians make "faith-based" alternatives. But what about good films that aren't explicitly Christian? What about historically based films that, though violent, remind us of courageous heroes and defining moments that changed the world? If Tom Cruise is in a movie, is it automatically a promo for Scientology?

Asking, "Where do I draw the line?"—called the *line approach* to culture—is too simplistic to be helpful. First, not everything labeled Christian is good, and not everything labeled secular is bad. Much that is labeled Christian—movies, songs, leaders, schools, churches, ministries, and organizations—fails to reach basic levels of excellence and honesty. And much that is labeled secular accurately portrays fallen humanity, displays artistic genius, and brings good to the world. As Gregory Thornbury, former president of The King's College, says, "'Christian' is the greatest of all possible nouns and lamest of all possible adjectives." It's meant to describe a person, not a thing.

An honest look at Christian history reveals we don't always draw lines in the right places. Not that long ago, some Christians drew lines between races by segregating Christian schools, condemning interracial marriages, and promoting other ways of keeping apart anyone who looked different than they did. Out-of-context Bible verses were used to prop up this sinful behavior. Mistakes like these prove just how susceptible Christians are to cultural pressure.

Line drawing is a shortsighted reaction to the cultural moment if not solidly grounded in the Christian Story. Of course, many behaviors and beliefs do "cross the line." The Bible speaks at length about how we should act, speak, and treat people. But that isn't the right question to ask *first*.

Starting with the Story

The apostle Peter was one of Jesus' closest friends. He walked with and learned directly from God's Son. When Peter wrote his first letter to Christ followers, it came during a difficult cultural moment. He referred to his audience—Christians scattered by a growing persecution—as "exiles." The persecution of Christ followers would only get worse, and Peter himself was eventually killed for his faith.

To strengthen the church in those trying times, the apostle, who famously denied Jesus, opened his letter not with the growing pressures and dangers of the moment but with a reminder of the gospel Story:

> Blessed be the God and Father of our Lord Jesus Christ! According to his great mercy, he has caused us to be born again to a living hope through the resurrection of Jesus Christ from the dead, to an inheritance that is imperishable, undefiled, and unfading, kept in heaven for you, who by God's power are being guarded through faith for a salvation ready to be revealed in the last time. (1 Pet. 1:3–5)

Only the good news of God's True Story of the world would enable Christ followers to endure trials, resist temptation, love their enemies, do good, and live well in the cultural moment. Peter didn't dwell on persecution or the pervasive immorality of pagan society. He returned again and again to the truth that defined their moment, our moment, and every moment of human history: Christ has risen from the dead! Our hope is secure.

The Bible Is One Big Story

Many Christians view the Scriptures in bits and pieces. Maybe you memorized individual Scripture verses or heard lots of Bible stories in Sunday school. If you just get bits and pieces, though, the Bible can become a disconnected collection of verses and stories designed to teach us how to be moral, happy, and successful.

Such a limited view of Scripture doesn't give us an accurate—or even exciting—story. A Hindu scholar once challenged the way Christian missionaries presented the Bible to people in India:

> I can't understand why you missionaries present the Bible to us in India as a book of religion. It is not a

book of religion—and anyway we have plenty of books of religion in India. We don't need any more! I find in your Bible a unique interpretation of universal history, the history of the whole of creation and the history of the human race.... That is unique. There is nothing else in the whole religious literature of the world to put alongside it.[3]

What we often miss is that the Bible is a comprehensive narrative. It tells the Story of the world, from the creation to the new creation.

Like all good stories, the biblical story line includes an introduction, a protagonist, antagonists, conflict, and resolution. Yet this Story is different from all other stories because it's God's Story. As such, it accurately describes reality, including what has gone wrong and how God will bring history to its final conclusion according to His purposes.

"What does this have to do with culture?" you may be asking.

Everything. If the Scriptures tell the true Story of the world, then our current cultural moment is part of its story line. The only way to make sense of what's happening at this moment is by placing it in its true context of God's bigger Story as recorded in the Bible.

The Bible is one big book made up of sixty-six smaller books and letters that dozens of people authored over thousands of years. Yet its Story, with all of its different characters, plotlines, twists, and turns, fits together and makes total sense. In fact, the Big Story of the Bible can be summarized in four chapters: creation, fall, redemption, and restoration.[4]

Creation

"In the beginning, God created the heavens and the earth" (Gen. 1:1).

That's how the Story begins. God is the author of the Story. The world we live in belongs to Him, not us. He is in charge. We are not. From the start, the Story established its *theology* (one God rules absolutely over everything) and its *cosmology* (the world is not an accident; it is an ordered creation). God, from the very beginning, was interested and engaged in the world He made. His plan was for it to flourish and be filled with life. And after each day of creation, God declared His world was good.

The pinnacle of the Story's first chapter is the creation of man and woman. God's plan for the world would be carried out by His image bearers. They were to "be fruitful and multiply and fill the earth and subdue it." And they were to "have dominion over the fish of the sea and over the birds of the heavens and over every living thing that moves on the earth" (Gen. 1:28). It wasn't their world; it was God's world. They were to care for it and cultivate it so that it would become the place God intended it to be. This is the Story's *anthropology*. The world God made, *and the capacity humans have to make something of the world*, were good from the beginning (see verses 18 and 31).

Of course, the next chapter affirms that there is bad in the world. But remember, the Story begins in Genesis 1—not Genesis 3.

Fall

In all good stories, something goes wrong. The big bad wolf gobbles up Grandma. The White Witch turns Narnia into a place where it is always winter but never Christmas. Sauron amasses an army of Orcs, goblins, trolls, bad wizards, and other evil creatures to conquer Middle-earth.

The biblical Story is no different. When Satan deceives Adam and Eve and they decide to follow their own path—instead of God's command— sin and death enter the Story. Order was disordered. Our good, God-given capacities were marred by evil acts, broken relationships, and selfish intentions. And we're part of the problem too. Sin is not just "out there," as if we're innocent bystanders. It's "in here," in every human heart and mind.

Yet even after sin and death entered the world, God never removed the expectation He had of His image bearers to be image bearers. His created intent that humans "be fruitful and multiply and fill the earth and subdue it" remained (Gen. 1:28). To be sure, the fruitful part is now accomplished only through the pains of childbirth, and thorns frustrate the subduing part. But the command to fill and subdue the earth still stands.

God created the world good, as well as our abilities to make something of it. As the apostle Paul told Timothy, God even "richly provides us with everything to *enjoy*" (1 Tim. 6:17). All is not lost.

Redemption

Thankfully, the biblical Story doesn't end after Genesis 2. The majority of the Story, in fact, is dedicated to redemption. God covers Adam and Eve's nakedness. He saves Noah's family from the flood, even as He wiped wickedness from the face of the earth. He creates a nation, Israel, to be His people. He preserves Israel despite their sin and rebellion, so that through them, all the nations of the earth would be blessed.

Redemption ultimately culminates in the person and work of Jesus Christ, the Word made flesh. He is light, and He is life (John 1:4). Jesus is, as Paul said, "the last Adam" (1 Cor. 15:45), righteous and obedient, though we are not. He took on the sin of the world, suffered God's wrath in our place, and ultimately defeated death by rising from the grave. All who embrace Christ are forgiven and become the children of God.

If that's all Christ accomplished, it would be enough to demand our worship and allegiance. But there's more. The Story did not end at Christ's resurrection, or at our redemption. There is a fourth chapter.

Restoration

Christians have long debated the details of how the biblical Story ends. However, the final chapter of the Story is summarized in the words of Christ Himself with a present-tense verb: "Behold, I am making all things new" (Rev. 21:5).

The Story that began with the creation of the heavens and the earth ends with a new beginning. The garden is restored in the midst of God's city. As the Old Testament prophet Ezekiel promised (Ezek. 37:27), the God who once walked with Adam and Eve will make His home with His people. "He will dwell with them, and they will be his people, and God himself will be with them as their God" (Rev. 21:3). When He makes His home with us, all wrongs will be made right, and all lies will be exposed as untrue.

A Better First Question

In God's Great Story, we live between redemption and restoration. Thankfully, before His ascension, Jesus offered instructions on how to live in this moment: "A new commandment I give to you," He said, "that you love one another: just as I have loved you, you also are to love one another" (John 13:34). We're to be disciples who make other disciples (Matt. 28:18–20). Paul tells children to obey their parents and husbands to love their wives. We should be good citizens, as Peter instructs (1 Pet. 2:13–15). And we're to wait expectantly for the culmination of the Story, which will occur when Christ returns (Rom. 8:22–24).

There are many more instructions in God's Word, but two especially deserve our attention here. First, as Peter wrote to the exiles facing their tough cultural moment, we are to be defined by hope (1 Pet. 3:15). This isn't a squishy, wishful-thinking, things-aren't-that-bad sort of optimism. The believer's hope, secured through the resurrection of Jesus Christ, isn't swayed by fickle feelings; it stands strong against the challenges of our times.

Second, the New Testament employs all kinds of "re-" words to describe life between redemption and restoration: renew, repent, restore, regeneration, reconciliation. Paul offered a mission statement to those who have been made new in Christ: "All this is from God, who through Christ reconciled us to himself and gave us the ministry of reconciliation" (2 Cor. 5:18). Reconciled ones are to be reconcilers.

Through faith, love, hope, and reconciliation, we can live God's Story in this moment without allowing culture to shape us. Only in the larger context of God's Story are the challenges we face in today's culture given proper perspective. That's why there's a better first question with which to approach culture than "Where do we draw the line?"

The better question is: "What is our salvation for?"

Chapter Three

A Vision of Success

*"Should one go off and build a little house with flowers outside the windows
and a garden outside the door and extol and thank God and turn one's
back on the world and its filth? Isn't seclusion a form of treachery—of
desertion? ... I'm weak and puny, but I want to do what is right."*

Hans Scholl, in a letter to Rose Naegele

"Somebody, after all, had to make a start."[1]

Sophie Scholl was just twenty-one years old when she spoke these words.
On February 22, 1943, she stood in front of the chief justice of the People's
Court of the Greater German Reich. He held her life in his hands. She refused
to back down. The Nazi chief justice convicted Sophie, her brother Hans, and
their friend Christoph Probst of treason and sent them to the guillotine.

Hans Scholl led the underground resistance movement known as the
White Rose. From June 1942 until their arrest, Hans, Sophie, and several
other University of Munich students secretly wrote and distributed anti-Nazi
pamphlets. Once they were discovered, punishment for their crimes was swift.
Within four days, they were detained, accused, tried, convicted, and executed.

Raised in a nominally religious German home, the Scholl siblings came
to a real, personal faith in Christ while at their university. In *The Fabric of
Faithfulness*, Steven Garber describes how their conversions motivated their
actions:

> Brother and sister began to find a place to stand. Reading
> the Scriptures in the light of the challenges presented by

their culture, having conversations with friends about the world and their place in it, meeting older, wiser people who offered them their time and their books— together they molded a vision about what was real and true and right.[2]

Many Germans, including those who followed Christ, chose to remain silent. They did nothing to resist Hitler and the Nazi regime. Others embraced the evil Nazi ideology. But the Scholl siblings' faith drove them from the sidelines. These students stood against the powerful German empire. Hans was supposed to meet Dietrich Bonhoeffer, a Christian pastor and perhaps the most famous figure of the German resistance, but never did. Instead, Hans was executed the very day the meeting was scheduled to take place.

Hans and Sophie had more in common with Bonhoeffer than a disgust with Nazi beliefs and actions. Whether they knew it or not, they also shared Bonhoeffer's Christ-shaped vision for culture, which might be summarized this way: "We are Christians, and we are Germans; therefore we are responsible for Germany."[3]

What Is Your Salvation For?

Christians often talk about how Christ saved us *from* sin and judgment, and *to* righteousness and eternal life with God. And those are really important truths to understand. The Scholl siblings, however, grasped a vision that they were saved *for* something too. Specifically, they believed that God had saved them *for* that particular moment in German history.

They were both Christian *and* German, and the intersection between the two meant they had a responsibility to do something. Before you decide how you will deal with culture, you need to know your responsibility as a Christ follower. In other words, what is your salvation for?

Called for the World, Not from It

This world is a broken place. But it's not a bad place. Gnosticism, a philosophy that has taken various forms throughout the history of the church, divides reality into two parts: the physical (which is evil) and the spiritual (which is good). Therefore, we should pursue sacred things (spiritual) and avoid that which is secular (physical).

However, as the previous chapter points out, the Bible describes the world differently. Because the world is both physical and spiritual—made "good" by God's hand before it was corrupted by human hands—reality is divided not between physical and spiritual but between the Creator and the creation. Though fallen, God's creation still proclaims His greatness, goodness, and love. Human activity, such as building, producing, selling, creating, cleaning, or any other work we do, should be seen as God's work.

Living in this good-yet-fallen place means living in tension. Sin and evil have thoroughly infected this beautiful world. People have profound capacities not only for justice, kindness, and love but also for injustice, cruelty, and hate. The Nazi officials who sent Jewish children to the gas chambers of Auschwitz during the day went home and hugged their own children at night.

Two reactions tempt Christians in every generation. The first is to run away from culture. Shouldn't we withdraw into the safety of the church, take care of our own, and avoid the darkness?

The other reaction is simply to avoid controversial issues. This way, we're told, we can keep the focus on God's love for all people. Both of these reactions offer ways to *escape* the tension.

But Christianity is not an escapist religion. At the center of Christianity is Jesus Christ. He didn't run from the world. He's the God who was born into the world and "moved into the neighborhood" (John 1:14 THE MESSAGE). God didn't send laws, prophets, angels, or a book to fix the world. Instead, He Himself came in the person of Jesus Christ.

The night before Jesus' crucifixion, He prayed for His disciples: "I do not ask that you take them out of the world, but that you keep them from the evil one" (John 17:15). In fact, the larger context of the prayer makes clear that Jesus' greatest desire for His disciples—"that they know you, the only true God, and Jesus Christ whom you have sent"—would happen not by escaping the world but as they lived in it (John 17:3).

God's people can still make a difference in the world! Proverbs 29:2 says, "When the righteous increase, the people rejoice, but when the wicked rule, the people groan." Even while the Israelites were exiled in a pagan land, God instructed His people through the prophet Jeremiah to live as they had in Israel:

> Build houses and live in them; plant gardens and eat their produce. Take wives and have sons and daughters; take wives for your sons, and give your daughters in marriage, that they may bear sons and daughters; multiply there, and do not decrease. But seek the welfare of the city where I have sent you into exile, and pray to the LORD on its behalf, for in its welfare you will find your welfare. (Jer. 29:5–7)

God created His image bearers to rule His good world on His behalf. Once we are redeemed and made right with God, we aren't immediately whisked away to heaven. That raises the question: *So now what?*

Should we hide in our holy huddles? No way! Christ didn't save us from being human; He saved us from our sins so that we would be fully human again.

The Story in Scriptures makes it clear that just as God intended His image bearers to bring life to the world by ruling over it, He also intends redeemed humans to join His work in bringing new life to the world. That's why Paul gave believers the mission statement of "the ministry of reconciliation" (see 2 Cor. 5:17–21).

Of course, the fall brought evil and brokenness into the world. Our best efforts and intentions don't always result in the best outcomes. Bad things happen to good people. Still, our salvation means we have work to *do now*, in God's redemptive plan for the world.

Writing from Tegel prison on July 21, 1944, Dietrich Bonhoeffer described how he had come to this understanding of Christianity in his own faith journey:

> During the last year or so, I've come to know and understand more and more the profound this-worldliness of Christianity.... I'm still discovering right up to this moment, that it is only by living completely in this world that one learns to have faith.[4]

Called to Our Times, Not Another

Not only are we called to the world; we're also called to a particular time and place. The apostle Paul bluntly stated this in his interaction with Epicurean and Stoic philosophers on Mars Hill in Athens, Greece:

> The God who made the world and everything in it, being Lord of heaven and earth, does not live in temples made by man, nor is he served by human hands, as though he needed anything, since he himself gives to all mankind life and breath and everything. And he made from one man every nation of mankind to live on all the face of the earth, having determined allotted periods and the boundaries of their dwelling place, that they should seek God, and perhaps feel their way toward him and find him. Yet he is actually not far from each one of us. (Acts 17:24–27)[5]

God is in charge of this cultural moment, and you can't escape it. Living in the West today requires that you talk about certain things, including topics you'd rather avoid. Not only is it impossible to escape our cultural situation, but God asks you to do the opposite. Christians should see their culture as the setting for living out their God-given calling to bring life to His world.

Too many Christians, especially in the wake of all of the recent cultural shifts, think it's hopeless to engage culture. "It's all over," they say. Some spiritualize their surrender by suggesting the culture-changing business gets in the way of the people-loving business. But you can't love people by ignoring the cultural evils that victimize them.

Others retreat, looking for safety. They believe that Christians should get out of the way and wait for God's judgment. "*We* tried to warn *them*," they say, "but *they* didn't listen."

That's not God's approach. Safety is never the goal for the Christ follower. Faithfulness is.

Could culture get worse? Yep. Remember, however, that we aren't the first Christ followers to face a difficult, or even seemingly hopeless, cultural moment. Plenty of Christians have had it worse. Believers throughout history, starting with John the Baptist, lost their lives for speaking truth. Like depressed and disillusioned Elijah after his great victory against the prophets of Baal (see 1 Kings 18–19), we're tempted to think we're alone. But Elijah wasn't, and neither are we. Those who run the race to engage the world join the "great cloud of witnesses" who have gone before (see Heb. 11–12).

And remember, there's much good that can be done. It's tempting to lose hope because of what's pouring out of Washington, DC; New York City; Hollywood; Paris; London. Of course, God has His people in those cities too. And we must use our positive influence where we can—like sports teams, clubs, youth groups, social-media platforms, classrooms, art studios, and theater companies. These places matter as well.

In the World but Not of It

Still, let's not fool ourselves. There are a lot of casualties in our culture. Church friends go to college and abandon their faith. Christians cave to cultural pressures. Pastors, fathers, wives, teenagers, and Christian celebrities blow it morally or suddenly announce they've changed their minds on long-held biblical views to avoid being on "the wrong side of history."

Our own sinful nature, plus the subtle but powerful influences in our culture, makes us susceptible to drifting into compromise. Smaller compromises lead to bigger ones. Even King Solomon, the wisest man of all time and builder of God's first temple, found his heart turned toward other gods (1 Kings 11).

So, how will you respond when the cultural pressure is on? How do you avoid becoming a cultural casualty? How can you be *in* the world but not *of* the world?

We need an all-encompassing vision of life that demands our deepest allegiance and grounds our identity. This requires more than just weekly Sunday school lessons, regular attendance at your youth group's midweek program, or a few summer mission trips. It requires a total transformation.

Following Jesus involves not only our beliefs and lifestyle but also our habits, attitudes, and affections. It's not enough to believe in God and be nice, yet keep Him closed off from most of our everyday lives. It's not enough to sprinkle a little Christian truth here and there if our lives are shaped more by the culture than the gospel. We need more than a pick-and-choose-what-makes-me-happy approach to the Christian life. We need a thorough, holistic, comprehensive, complete, and total Christian world and life view. And what does that look like?

Years ago, a twentysomething dragged her friend up to talk to me (John) at a conference where I was speaking.

"Thank you for saying that we need more Christian fashion designers," she said.

"You're welcome," I responded and inwardly panicked because I didn't even remember saying that, nor had I ever really thought much about a Christian view of fashion.

Thankfully she had more to say about it than I did: "My friend here is moving up the ladder as a fashion designer, and I tell her all the time how important her work is. Fashion designers teach culture what is beautiful."

That's exactly right. When mature Christians engage the culture fully, deeply, and wisely, the culture won't corrupt us. Just the opposite. We'll change the culture. We'll put on display what is good, true, and beautiful.

For two thousand years, many of the highest and best artifacts of culture have come from Christians—whether Dante's *The Divine Comedy*, Gutenberg's printing press, Bach's music, T. S. Eliot's poetry, Arthur Guinness's innovative business culture, Flannery O'Connor's novels, Truett Cathy's chicken sandwich (thanks, Chick-fil-A!), Makoto Fujimura's paintings, Joni Eareckson Tada's care for the disabled, and so many more. Now, it's your turn.

So what is cultural success? It's a life lived like Hans and Sophie Scholl. It's a life deeply engaged in the moment in which God has placed us, where we courageously navigate the threatening currents and know that we serve a cause, and a God, far greater than ourselves.

Part Two

The Dangerous Undercurrents of Our Culture

Chapter Four

The Information Age

"We are drowning in information, while starving for wisdom."
E. O. Wilson

Historians not only study past eras; they name them. We learn about the Roaring Twenties, the Middle Ages, and the Industrial Revolution. Our current era has already been identified. We live in the Information Age.

According to Wikipedia (where else would you find a definition for this?), the Information Age is "characterized by the shift from traditional industry … to an economy based on information computerization."[1] This is a complicated way of saying that our world is no longer dominated by farms and factories but by glowing screens.

Older generations may remember life before 24/7 access to the internet. But you've never known a quiet world. Every day of your life, you encounter more information than people who lived in the fifteenth century would have over the course of their entire lives. Each day, 500 million tweets are sent, 4 million hours of content are uploaded to YouTube, 4.3 billion Facebook messages are posted, 6 billion Google searches are conducted, and 205 billion emails are sent.[2] In just about every restaurant, every store, and every room in most homes, music is blaring and screens are on.

Life in the Information Age is noisy, and it only becomes noisier as the competition grows fiercer for your ears, eyes, and money. Information technology can make life convenient and more efficient. But be careful not to confuse information with knowledge or knowledge with wisdom.[3]

It's Not Just Information

The world you live in could also be called the age of ideas. Every song, movie, tweet, Snap, sermon, news story, podcast, banner ad, and billboard tells us something about what to believe and how to live. Even information you think is unimportant to you communicates ideas about life and the world.

Ideas are sometimes true and sometimes false. They may be good or bad, shallow or significant. Ideas influence the way we think and live. Ideas take various forms, but they must be taken seriously. Why? Because *ideas have consequences*. They shape entire societies and drive the course of human history.

And that's why *bad ideas* have victims. Real people, including innocent bystanders, suffer the consequences of bad ideas. For young women, bad ideas about popularity, physical appearance, and your value as a person leave you confused, anxious, and depressed. Have you ever felt "less than" or left out when scrolling through your friends' Instagram feeds? For young men, bad ideas about masculinity can stunt your maturity, leaving you content to wander aimlessly through your teens and twenties, dodging responsibility and rationalizing your addiction to video games. Bad ideas about sex and relationships fuel the hookup culture on college campuses, leaving you broken, used, and lonely.

Ideas are particularly difficult to navigate today. Because ideas can come at you quickly and from many directions, it can be difficult to recognize them, much less think critically about them. This is no small problem. If we can't master ideas, ideas will master us.

It would be helpful, of course, if ideas came with warnings. Movies, television shows, songs, and YouTube videos have disclaimers about foul language, explicit sexuality, and excessive violence. Ideas come with no such warnings. But if they did, the disclaimer might look something like this:

The following (song, movie, show, commercial, speech,
tweet, post, image, story, book, sermon, etc.) contains

ideas in the form of arguments, embodied characters, narrative consequences, satirical exaggerations, and/or emotional outbursts. These ideas will be assumed true, though not necessarily supported by any arguments, and reflect the worldview of the actors, producers, directors, musicians, writers, or speakers. Discretion is advised.

Struggling with Ideas

Making sense of ideas in a culture of information overload isn't easy. For starters, you often cannot control which ideas you will be exposed to, or when. Access and exposure to new ideas are just a swipe away. Even if you're not looking for reasons to question your faith, non-Christian ideas about God, truth, and morality are looking for you.

That's why it's critical to build a firm foundation by asking tough questions about faith from your parents, church leaders, and mentors. Dive into your beliefs. Don't be afraid to wrestle with controversial topics. It isn't wrong to ask questions.

Doubting isn't sinning. If it is indeed wrong to question God, the book of Psalms needs to be taken out of the Bible. As you read through Israel's hymnbook, notice how many times David or another psalmist wonders aloud whether God was truly good—or even there at all.

Of course, honest questions differ significantly from cynicism. In Proverbs, Solomon distinguished between those who seek God and those who mock Him. Mockers aren't interested in answers. Seekers are. The hearts of mockers are so hard, they'd reject the truth even if was staring them in the face. Keeping an open heart and mind is key.

Oftentimes seekers become mockers if they're *not* allowed to wrestle with doubts and questions. In the Information Age, your questions should be taken seriously. At the same time, don't expect your parents, pastors, or other trusted adults in your life to have all the answers. If they respond to one of your questions with "I really don't know, but let's find an answer together," then join them on that journey.

One of the biggest challenges in the Information Age is discovering *who to trust* and *who to journey with through life*. You have to decide who to believe: your pastor or your professor? Who knows more: your parents or your peers? Where should you search for answers: Google or Galatians?

The issue of trust can become complicated as you see hypocrisy in the church or in your home. A student (let's called her Jenny) once approached me (John) after a conference and asked the classic question: "Why does God let bad things happen to good people?"

Ready with a rational answer, I jumped into explanations about human freedom, resurrection hope, and the failure of other worldviews to explain evil or good.

As soon as I finished my argument, Jenny looked at me with tears in her eyes and said, "That doesn't help me." She explained how she had been deeply disappointed by the moral failure of her dad and how the church he pastored had mistreated her family. "I'm mad," Jenny continued. "I'm mad at my dad because he let me down. I'm mad at the church because they stabbed us in the back. And I'm mad at God because He let all of this happen."

Like so many people, Jenny's intellectual doubt was an outward expression of an internal hurt. She stopped trusting God because the people she trusted let her down.

It's often been said that the main problem with Christianity is Christians. That's true in as far as we still sin, still fail, and still hurt others. After all, perfect people aren't Christians; forgiven people are. On the other hand, nothing strengthens faith more than seeing Christ restore a broken life, marriage, or relationship. So, we can still trust and hope because we have a heavenly Father who guides, forgives, restores, and rescues. And that's what the third chapter of God's True Story—redemption—is all about.

As you live in and engage the culture, you must learn how and why to trust God's Story, revealed in the Bible. It's easy to accept the Scriptures at church or at home in an environment where everyone basically agrees that it's the Word of God. It's much more difficult to trust the Bible on a college campus or in some other environment where the Bible is seen as racist or homophobic (see chapter 16 for a better understanding of the authority of Scripture).

In the Information Age, you will encounter objections to the Bible and serious challenges to the Christian faith. An aggressive and hostile world won't let you slide by; you have to think your way through this culture. Without an understanding of basic logic, even the weakest arguments can sideline you.

For example, do you know the difference between an *assertion* and an *argument*? The statement "The Genesis account is one of many creation myths in ancient literature, so it cannot be true" is *not* an argument. It's an assertion, a claim that needs to be investigated and clarified to see if it holds water. *In what ways is the biblical account similar to myths? In what ways is it different? Which came first?*

But clarity alone doesn't turn an assertion into an argument, let alone a strong and persuasive one. A good argument must be supported with reasons and evidence. *What's the evidence the biblical writers copied other ancient myths? If two accounts are similar, does it follow they're both false? Which stories have the backing of authoritative sources?*

Also, don't confuse feelings for reasons. Feeling isn't thinking, but a lot of people can't tell the difference. We're constantly told that being nice is more important than being right, and that affirming someone's "truth" is better than knowing *the* truth. As a result, our culture has no idea what it means to be tolerant. True tolerance means you treat others with respect even if their views differ from yours. In today's world, however, if you don't embrace and even celebrate the views of the majority culture, you're considered a hate-filled bigot. In a culture like this, people are pressured not to think but to conform.

Also stunting our ability to think are distractions by different forms of entertainment. Way back in 1985, social critic Neil Postman wrote a book accusing Americans of "amusing ourselves to death."[4] The word *amuse* literally means "not to think" (*muse* is to think, and the *a* at the front negates it). Too much amusement from entertainment stunts our ability to think. (Chapter 13 examines entertainment more closely.)

Those who can't think clearly in the Information Age are easy targets for false ideas and deception. We must know enough, and care enough, to make sense of the ideas we encounter. As the apostle Paul instructed his readers, "See to it that no one takes you captive by philosophy and empty deceit" (Col. 2:8).

Thinking "Worldviewishly"

In a world of bad ideas, we need good ideas. Knowing what is true is always important. But if true information is merely added to the flood of information, it can be drowned out. Like a drop of water in the ocean, truth can be overwhelmed with lies, half-truths, propaganda, or trivialities.

Because of all the noise and distractions in our lives, we need to not only *hear* truth, but we also need to learn what it means to *think* with truth. Check out this prayer from Paul for the church at Philippi:

> It is my prayer that your love may abound more and more, with knowledge and all discernment, so that you may approve what is excellent, and so be pure and blameless for the day of Christ, filled with the fruit of righteousness that comes through Jesus Christ, to the glory and praise of God. (Phil. 1:9–11)

What Paul offered is a terrific description of discernment. In his prayer, *discernment* is "the ability to *distinguish* the true and genuine from the false and counterfeit." To rise above all the noise and live well in this culture, discernment is required. We must develop the ability to not only recognize the truth but also to see all of life through the truth.

As we said earlier, everyone has a worldview, or a set of "belief glasses," through which we see the world. We don't look *at* our worldview; we look *through* it. It's the story through which we see and make sense of the real world.

We all have foundational beliefs about the nature of reality— whether the world is an accident of nature or a purposeful creation of God, whether right and wrong are objective or a matter of personal preference, whether there is or isn't an afterlife, whether humans are just more evolved animals or an altogether unique kind of being with some sort of privileged place in the universe.

The question isn't whether you have a worldview. The question is: Which worldview has you?

Worldviews are caught more than taught. Like a cold, most people "catch" their worldview beliefs from the culture around them. If you never stop and examine your worldview, you'll still have one, but it may not be the right one.

Your worldview should answer the big and most significant questions in life, like:

- Origin: Where did everything come from?
- Identity: What is a human being? Who am I?
- Meaning: What is the meaning of life? What is my purpose?
- Morality: Is there right and wrong, and if so, who determines it? What's wrong with the world, and how can it be fixed?
- Destiny: What happens when I die? Where is history headed?

Forgive the double negative, but you can't *not* answer these questions. If you don't take time to answer them in your heart and mind, you'll answer them passively by how you live, how you make decisions, and especially, how you relate to others.

For example, if there is no God who created the world (origin), then humans are just accidental by-products of natural forces (identity), with no ultimate purpose to their lives (meaning). From this kind of world-view, it follows that two students involved in one of the most infamous school shootings in American history, Columbine High School shooters Dylan Klebold and Eric Harris, were correct in their belief that there is no life after death (destiny), and therefore, they faced no eternal conse-quences for their actions on April 20, 1999, that killed thirteen people (morality).

Our view *of* the world provides the framework, or story, by which we make sense of what happens *in* the world. If life has no ultimate purpose, then neither does suffering. If humans are nothing more than biological machines, then our value is reduced to what we look like or what we can do. If there is no designer of the universe, then concepts like marriage, sexuality, and government are whatever we decide they are.

Shaping Worldview

Our worldview also determines our view *for* the world. Our worldview shapes our values, and our values shape our behavior. Remember, ideas have consequences.

Despite all the noise of our culture, we can still form a robust and thoughtful Christian worldview. Here's how.

1. Start building a Christian worldview. If God's Story is the true story about reality, then we must know *what* it is we believe. How does the Christian worldview answer the big questions of origin, identity, mean-ing, morality, and destiny? Our answers will build the foundation of our worldview.

2. Think regularly about your worldview. Every song, movie, televi-sion program, article, speech, tweet, post, and commercial reflect values and behavior rooted in a worldview. Compare the messages contained in entertainment to what you know from the truth in the Bible. By thinking worldviewishly about *everything*, you'll become an active participant in developing your worldview, rather than simply absorbing cultural views.

3. Learn about non-Christian worldviews. When ideas are named, they're far less intimidating or powerful. Develop the ability to identify worldviews when you encounter them.

I (John) received an email from Chris, a student who attended a Summit worldview conference I led. In the email, Chris described how going to a movie with his friends was different now that he had learned about worldviews. "I tried to veg out during the movie, but I just couldn't. As I watched it, I kept thinking, *Wait a minute, that's secular humanism, and wait a minute, that's not true. And what do they mean by that, and how do they know that's true?* I learned that I just can't turn this worldview thing off!" After the movie, he was able to discuss with his friends the ideas he had spotted in the film. "They thought it was really cool," he said, "and wanted to know how I was able to see all the things in the movie that I did."[5]

4. Read good books. The saying is true: "Leaders are readers, and readers are leaders." When you read good books, you not only learn good things, but you also learn to think. Reading will mature your mind like nothing else.

5. Discuss ideas whenever possible. If a song lyric catches your attention in a store, talk to your parents about it. If a commercial promises that a product will bring fulfillment, talk about it with your friends. Pause a movie and discuss the difference between the good guys and the bad guys. Opportunities to talk about ideas are everywhere.

6. Ask good questions. The two best educators in history, Jesus and Socrates, were great question askers. There is no better way to make your friends wrestle with ideas than through dialogue. Here are a few simple questions to keep handy:

- *What do you mean by that?* The battle of ideas begins with the battle for definitions. Often you'll find that even if you're using the same vocabulary as others, you aren't using the same dictionary.

- *How do you know that's true?* Assertions require arguments. This question will not only force someone to back up what they say, but it will also help them identify unsupported claims. Of course, your friends will quickly learn to toss this question back at you! If you don't have good reasons for what you believe, don't worry. Tell them you'll do more research and get back to them. Encourage them to do the same with their beliefs. Then ask your parent, youth pastor, or trusted mentor to help you find the truth.

- *Why does it matter?* This question gets at the consequences of ideas. Blaise Pascal famously proposed a "wager" about God. If Christians are wrong and atheists are right about God, nothing is eternally lost. However, if Christians are right, then atheists will face eternal consequences for their unbelief.

Care about truth and seek after it. Dig into ideas. Hold on to what's true. Build your worldview. Ask questions. Turn to your parents or a wise adult for help. Developing a Christian worldview, rooted in Scripture, will prepare you to navigate the age of information.

Chapter Five

The Loss of Identity

"The idols of the nations are silver and gold, the work of human hands.
They have mouths, but do not speak; they have eyes, but do not see; they
have ears, but do not hear, nor is there any breath in their mouths. Those
who make them become like them, so do all who trust in them."
Psalm 135:15–18

In an April 2013 *Sports Illustrated* article, NBA center Jason Collins announced to the world that he was gay. It became a major news story. At the time, the big-three professional sports leagues (the NBA, NFL, and MLB) were largely untouched by the LGBTQ (lesbian, gay, bisexual, transgender, queer) revolution.

The response was almost universally positive. President Obama called Collins with his personal congratulations, and the First Lady tweeted, "We've got your back." Basketball legends, celebrities, and media praised the announcement as historic and groundbreaking. The most common reaction was: "Finally, Jason Collins can be himself" or "He no longer has to hide who he is."

Following the announcement, NBA analyst Chris Broussard faced a number of questions about the story's implications on the ESPN show *Outside the Lines*: Would more players now come out as gay? How would his teammates react? Would teams shy away from signing Collins, who had been a solid role player throughout his career? It was a fascinating conversation.

Then it got personal.

Broussard, who is open about his own Christian faith, was asked about something that had nothing to do with basketball: Did he agree with Collins's claim that there was no conflict between his Christian faith and living as a sexually active gay man? Broussard answered,

> Personally I don't believe that you can live an openly homosexual lifestyle or an openly ... like premarital sex between heterosexuals [sic].... If you're openly living that type of lifestyle, then the Bible says "you know them by their fruits." It says that, you know, that's a sin.... And if you're openly living in unrepentant sin, whatever it may be, not just homosexuality—adultery, fornication, premarital sex between heterosexuals—whatever it may be, I believe that's walking in open rebellion to God and to Jesus Christ. So I would not characterize that person as a Christian because I don't think the Bible would characterize them as a Christian.[1]

You can imagine what happened next. Critics demanded that Broussard resign or be fired. They said he was an intolerant bigot who clearly hated homosexuals.

If you look carefully at what Broussard said, he didn't just single out Collins but condemned the sexual behavior of many players in the NBA. However, an outspoken minority of people loudly proclaimed that his views on homosexuality were unacceptable, that Broussard should have known that hateful and bigoted views like his are to be kept out of public conversation, even if he was directly asked to share them. For them, being a Christian and holding the views of popes, pastors, theologians, and leaders—not to mention a significant portion of the American population—are no excuse.

When Jason Collins announced his sexuality, he was encouraged to share *his* truth. But Chris Broussard was told that his Christian faith amounted to little more than a personal opinion he should keep to himself.

The Cultural Identity Crisis

The Jason Collins story illustrates how our culture is caught up in an identity crisis. Sex used to be talked about in terms of behavior. It was something you did. Now it's "who you are." Your sexual desires and attractions define you. In today's culture, sexuality can be your identity.

Sexuality is confused with identity because our culture has lost what it means to be human. And our changing answers to this important worldview question will have dramatic consequences.

Imagine a car company stockpiling engines, steering wheels, bumpers, tires, seat covers, and other parts, intending to launch a new line of automobiles.

"What kind of cars will you build?" you ask the CEO. "Full size or midsize? What will they look like when they're finished?"

"No idea," he replies. "We'll just throw the parts together and see what happens." Yeah, those cars won't work very well, will they? A carmaker with no clear idea on what a car is, is a company without a promising future.

In the same way, if you don't know what it really means to be human—what you are, what your purpose is, and why you are here in the first place—then you're left to make up your own answers. All you can do is throw "parts" together. Identity becomes whatever you want it to be. Race, class, interests, hobbies, accomplishments, and even sexuality are the categories we now use to represent who we are to the world.

A carmaker with no idea what a car is can't make cars that function properly. The result? Broken-down cars. Likewise, people with no idea what a human being is (the Big Story), can't tell us how we should properly live our lives. The result? Broken-down human beings.

Welcome to identity after Christianity.

Christianity has contributed many things to the world, but none more important than its vision of the human person. As atheist philosopher Luc Ferry describes it, "Christianity was to introduce the notion that ... men were equal in dignity—an unprecedented idea at the time, and one to which our world owes its entire democratic inheritance."[2]

Human dignity and equality are concepts everyone accepts today. But most forget that they grew out of the Judeo-Christian doctrine of the *imago Dei* ("image of God"), the biblical vision that God created humans specially and uniquely, endowing them with eternal value. Many people want the fruit of human dignity while soundly condemning its Christian roots. That just doesn't work.

As the twentieth century demonstrated through war, violence, ethnic cleansing, and human bloodshed, severing human dignity from its Christian roots is foolish, even deadly. God made us in His image. We can only know ourselves if we know God. And without God, we no longer know who we are. Human life becomes just a bunch of random nerve endings and reflexes with no real purpose.

The twenty-first century, having inherited that twentieth-century baggage, is full of contradiction. We want human rights without knowing what a human is. Students are educated with *whats* and *hows* but offered no coherent vision of *why*. Some babies are dramatically protected, operated on, and saved in the womb, while other babies are targeted for abortion, particularly those with disabilities.

Human culture wants to flourish without God. But it won't happen. As society rejects God, it chooses instead to worship modern idols:

Self. The first of the Ten Commandments is "You shall have no other gods before [Me]" (Ex. 20:3). Today we have no other gods before *me*.

State. The apostle Paul wrote, "My God will supply every need" (Phil. 4:19). Today people increasingly look to government to supply their needs.

Sex. God gave this very good gift to us as a means of expressing love and marital oneness. Today it's many people's highest pursuit, an end in and of itself.

Science. God created an orderly and intricate universe. Today the word of science (or, more accurately, of scientists) has replaced the Word of God as the source of truth and knowledge.

Stuff. Blaise Pascal famously wrote of a God-shaped void we all have that only God can fill.[3] Today the constant barrage of commercials and marketing slogans proclaims that the void in our heart is stuff-shaped.

Idols can never replace God. Instead they dehumanize us. The psalmist wrote, "Those who make [idols] become like them, so do all who trust in them" (Ps. 135:18). The truth is we see ourselves and others in the image of whatever it is we worship. For example, those who make sex an idol see people only as sexual objects, valued because of their appearance and used for pleasure. Christ followers view every individual with inherent dignity and value.

The cultural identity crisis also creates a personal identity crisis. As a student, you may especially struggle with who you are and why you're here. You might see your friends succumb to false identities, such as "I am what I can do" or "I am what others think I am" or "I am my sexual inclinations" or "I am what I look like." And you see and feel the effects. Sadness. Anxiety. Depression. Anger. Suicidal thoughts. Broken lives.

If we don't know what it means to be human, how can we know what it means to be Christian? Discipleship is the only antidote for this confusion. You must know not only what to believe and how to behave but also who you are as a redeemed image bearer of the Creator.

Who Are You, Really?

How can you form an identity, discerning the truth from the lies about what makes you who you are? These three areas are critical in contributing to identity formation: story, questions, and community.

Story

Think of the person you know better than anyone else in the world. Is it because you've memorized that person's weight, height, IQ, blood type, and SAT scores?

Of course not! We know people by their stories. When they tell us where they're from, what their families are like, and what they enjoy doing, they're revealing who they are by offering bits and pieces of their stories. Story and identity are intimately connected.

Many students don't know who they are largely because today's postmodern culture doesn't have a coherent story. Postmodernism rejects the existence of a universal Story of history and humanity.[4] But throughout the Old Testament, the psalmists and the prophets called Israel to obedience by telling and retelling the Story of how God chose, led, and rescued them as His people. The New Testament, particularly in the letters of Paul and Peter, consistently reminds the church of who they are as God's new people by telling and retelling the Story of how God, in Christ, chose, led, and rescued them as His people.

In a storyless culture, Christ followers must know the true Story of all reality. Christians often talk about, but rarely define, finding our "identity in Christ." Biblically speaking, however, we can't know our identity in Christ without knowing His Story as revealed in Scripture.

In chapter 2, we explained how the Story of Scripture is told in four chapters: creation, fall, redemption, and restoration. Each chapter reveals core truths about our identity as image bearers: we were created to make something of the world, ruling God's place for His glory (creation); we rebelled, human sin brought death into the world (fall); we were rescued by Jesus Christ, who exchanged His righteousness for our unrighteousness (redemption); we are called back to our full humanity as both messengers and agents of the risen Christ, who is "making all things new" (restoration). With this Story, the Bible frames all of reality—including our identity.

Questioning

A second area that's critical to forming your identity is asking difficult questions about God, life, and faith.

Canadian behavioral psychologist James Marcia has done extensive research on identity formation.[5] He identified four stages—*diffusion*, *foreclosure*, *moratorium*, and *achievement*—based on two critical questions: (1) Have you wrestled with life's big questions (i.e., origins, identity, meaning, morality, and destiny)? and (2) Have you committed to a particular vision of life based on your exploration of the alternatives?

- People in a state of *diffusion* have neither explored life's meaning nor made any commitments to a particular vision of life. They have no real sense of who they are.
- Those in *foreclosure* have committed to a vision of life without ever wrestling with the questions themselves. Instead, they embrace the vision of others—for example, their parents or their community.
- *Moratorium* describes those who constantly explore alternative visions of life but refuse to commit to any of them. Always questioning, they never settle on any answers.
- *Achievement* is the stage for those who have sufficiently wrestled with the big questions and have sufficiently committed to a vision of life. They know who they are and how they fit in the world.

Pause for a moment and ask, "What stage am I in?" Our culture often leaves students in perpetual *moratorium*, constantly barraging you with new ideas and information. You're continuously told to question everything, to explore every alternative, and to keep an open mind on everything from religion to gender. But if you're stuck in moratorium, you'll be incredibly unstable, prone to deception, disappointment, and cynicism.

On the other hand, Marcia's description of *foreclosure* describes Christian teenagers who've never wrestled with whether Christianity is, in fact, true. Maybe it's because they're living off their parents' faith. If you find yourself here, one atheist professor, sexual failure, or personal tragedy can cause you to lose your faith. Simply put, your worldview just isn't big enough for the challenges of the real world.[6]

It's crucial that you go to your parents or find a Christian mentor who can help you answer and understand life's biggest questions. By walking with a trusted adult who takes your questions and doubts seriously, you can discover your true identity. The capacity for curiosity and struggle is among God's greatest gifts to us. Yet the ultimate purpose of questioning isn't merely to question, nor is it to find answers and win arguments. Identity is found when you commit to a life in the service of Jesus, who is the way, the truth, and the life. Identity requires believing. It also requires belonging, so don't wrestle with these questions alone.

Community

The God who made us in His image is Himself an eternal community called the Trinity. This means He doesn't merely *do* relationships; He *is* a relationship. As His image bearers, we'll never know who we are in isolation from others.

This is why church isn't optional. It's the community of God to which we belong and with whom we're to live and serve. For the believer, there is no substitute for the church.

Maybe you've seen the statistics about older teens and college students dropping out of church. There are many reasons for this, but one is the tendency of churches to age-segregate their members. Often, we show up at church and completely separate ourselves. Children go to their class, youth to their program, and adults to "big church." Age-specific programming for children and youth can be helpful but often become a substitute for church, cutting us off from one another. This means you may miss out on wise adult mentors and fail to learn what it truly means to be part of a community you desperately need.

Don't be a statistic. Encourage your group of friends to attend church and engage in small-group Bible study. Get radical and ask your youth pastor to cancel the Sunday morning youth program so the students can worship side by side with the adults. We all need to be part of the church community from the beginning, developing relationships with all age groups, learning to serve, and participating in God's mission, *together*. You need the church, especially as you enter adulthood and start making so many critical life decisions.

And, it should be added, the church needs you too.

Chapter Six

Being Alone Together

"Not that long ago, we were trying to figure out how we would keep our computers busy.... [Now] they keep us busy. It's kind of as though we are their killer app."
Sherry Turkle, psychologist and professor

Have you ever been physically separated from your phone and sensed that you just received a text message? You're sitting in class while your phone is in your locker, and yet in some sort of strange violation of the space-time continuum, you know that you just received a text.

Most everybody has experienced "phantom ringing," a mental false alarm of receiving a call or a text message, but this is different. This is like a technological mind-reading. It's like your phone is somehow connected to your person.

Sherry Turkle is incredibly smart, a psychologist and professor of social studies and technology at the Massachusetts Institute of Technology (MIT). For the last thirty years she has studied the impact of computer and online technology on people and their relationships. She used to think technology would revolutionize our lives for the good. But after years of study and observation, she changed her tune.

Turkle recently wrote a book titled *Alone Together: Why We Expect More from Technology and Less from Each Other*. Instead of being optimistic about online life, she expresses a deep concern about the state of human relationships. She argues that as our technology increases, so does our loneliness, anxiety, and depression. Rather than bringing us together, the internet is wrecking our relationships. "We're designing technologies that will give us the illusion of companionship without the demands of friendship."[1]

How Our Technology Shapes Us

Historically, every new technology has naysayers who predict terrible things will happen to humanity if we don't resist it. Most of the time, technofears are overblown. However, it is concerning how much of our lives are now online and how it's affecting us.

If you're like most students, you tend to dramatically underestimate how much time you spend with phones, tablets, televisions, or computer monitors. The average time students spend in front of glowing screens continues to skyrocket. CNN recently reported that Americans now spend ten hours a day with screens of some kind.[2]

There is virtually no place in our lives where a screen isn't front and center. When was the last time you were hanging out with friends and not a single person took out a smartphone? Yeah, never. It's no exaggeration to say that relationships today are lived out more indirectly than directly. Today, our digital devices intrude on every experience, conversation, and relationship. And there are consequences when life is lived this way.[3] We're risking losing touch on multiple levels.

First, we lose touch with our world. Especially through social media like Snapchat, Twitter, and Instagram, we adopt an odd posture toward everyday life. Rather than enjoying the moment we're in and making the most of an experience, we find ourselves thinking, *How many likes and shares will my picture of this get?*

Second, we lose touch with one another. Because so much communication doesn't happen face to face, we struggle with basic people skills, like making eye contact in conversation or understanding nonverbal cues.

Online life also challenges our willingness and ability to be honest and vulnerable with others. We carefully curate our social-media profiles, meticulously editing every picture and post for friends and family to scroll through (and perhaps to be jealous of!). We don't post our struggles or lonely moments online. We present ourselves in the best possible way. This is largely responsible for ushering in the "age of envy." As we browse the pages of Instagram celebrities (or even friends), their lives seem way more desirable than ours.

Social media also fosters a false sense of intimacy and connection with others. Today we can have thousands of "friends." But in reality we lack deep, meaningful relationships. Jimmy Kimmel, in his frequent late-night-television-show segment called "Mean Tweets," demonstrates how technology allows us to dismiss the humanity of others. Kimmel will have celebrities, athletes, and other public figures read out loud terrible things people have tweeted at them, like:

- You look like someone who just gave up.
- You're the worst thing to ever happen. Full stop. #UghBarf
- Trying to imagine what's worse, you or Hitler.
- Here's how you could help your fellow humans. Disappear forever.

Clearly, we're far more likely to say things online than we'd ever say to someone's face.

Third, we lose touch with ourselves. The tendency today is to become curators of our own online museums. When we carefully select and edit images to share with others, we can lose touch with the real us as we construct a false identity.

Additionally, online life gives the false impression that we can separate who we are into public and private realms. Particularly in the case of pornography addiction (which is a problem for boys *and* girls), we cultivate deadly sins online under different identities. But there is only one self—a God-created one.

Over time, the pressures of our online platforms can even cause us to abandon our deeply held convictions. If you express Christian views on controversial issues like homosexuality, same-sex marriage, or transgender identity, your social status will take a big hit. So we just stay silent or even start to change our beliefs. Plus, we often feel required to like the post of a friend or celebrity, even if he or she is boasting about a view or activity that violates God's standards.

The Lies Technology Teaches Us

Dr. Kathy Koch, a popular speaker and an expert in educational psychology and learning styles, describes the lies that are taught by our tech-shaped culture.[4] Consider whether you and your friends have bought into these lies:

Lie #1: I am the center of my own universe.

Technology allows you to live in an online world of your own making. You design the playlists and photo albums according to your online personality. Google even tracks your online behavior and delivers custom search results it thinks you desire. Technology promises to cater to your every need, without limitations. Everything is designed to revolve around *you*.

Of course, reality doesn't always bend to your wants or needs. If you believe you're the center of your own universe, you're in for a world of hurt and disappointment. Even worse, you'll fall for the very first lie: "You will be like God, knowing good and evil" (Gen. 3:5).

Lie #2: I deserve to be happy all the time.

Today's technology promises immediate gratification. You can get what you want when you want it. It's an on-demand world: movies, music, sexual pleasure, adventure, violence, revenge, gadgets, games. If an app or game or platform doesn't satisfy, you simply move on to the next thing. It's ironic that with so many distractions and devices that so many students seem perpetually bored.

Scroll through Instagram. Pay close attention to your friends' Snapchat stories. What do you see? Smiling people going to cool places, eating great food, and having wonderful vacations. Technology teaches that the good life is one that's faster, easier, on your own terms, and full of pleasure. Online, everyone seems to be happy. And you deserve to be happy too.

However, real life includes lonely moments, hard work, dissatisfaction, struggle, and pain. But if everyone around you seems to be happy all the time and you're not, you'll be tempted to think there's something wrong with your life. No wonder anxiety and depression are on the rise in your generation. According to the Centers for Disease Control and Prevention (CDC), suicide is the second leading cause of death for ten- to twenty-four-year-olds.[5]

If you fall for this lie, you'll absorb the values of the culture—convenience, choice, and pleasure. But you'll miss developing essential character qualities that lead to true joy and contentment—patience, wisdom, and perseverance.

Lie #3: I must have choices.

Technology gives us the illusion that choices are required to be happy and fulfilled. You have an unlimited number of choices of movies, songs, games, tablets, phones, experiences, and relationships (real or virtual). Our online world is infinitely customizable too. Every website has a drop-down menu with more options. You can create and customize hundreds of playlists. Watch a single episode or binge an entire season on Netflix. You're in control of it all.

Choice, in and of itself, isn't bad, of course. But when so much of life is lived online, it's only a small jump to thinking that's the way all of reality should be as well. If you're trapped in the lie that choices are necessary prerequisites to happiness, two things result: First, rather than seizing the opportunities in front of you, you will always be looking for the next better thing. Second, addiction to choice leads to ungratefulness, never being satisfied with what you have. And a thankless heart is an unhappy one.

Lie #4: Information is all I need, not teachers.
Why ask for advice from others when you can just Google the answers to your questions? Why ask Mom and Dad, when Siri is always available? In the age of information, there's a huge temptation to ignore the wisdom of people around you or, worse, to think they don't have any. Gray hair used to indicate wisdom. Now it identifies someone who is out of touch.

But remember, don't confuse information with knowledge and completely forgo the pursuit of wisdom. A wise teacher, parent, youth leader, or mentor can help you separate the truth from error and pass along wisdom they've gained from years of experience. And the best teachers will help you to see everything in light of God's Story.

Avoid Being Alone Together

So how can you counter the tech tsunami engulfing your life? An obvious practical step is to limit screen time, especially with your smartphone. One way to do this is through a technology fast, a designated amount of time when you choose to go without something. Yes, we're serious! Take breaks from your phone, iPad, laptop, or television. Purposely unplug to gain control over your devices rather than have them control you.

Next, talk with your parents, friends, or an accountability partner about the idea and come up with a plan. Perhaps it's every day after dinner, Sunday afternoons, or one day a week. Use that time to read your Bible or a good book, spend time with family or friends, have face-to-face conversations, play games, play an instrument, paint, get outside, ride your bike, ride your skateboard, go on a hike, or do something active.

Here's another idea: establish device-free zones, times, and spaces where you unplug.

1. The car. Obviously, texting while driving is dangerous. More than that, however, rides to and from school, church, and shopping can be great times to connect with family, friends, and God.

2. The dinner table. Talk to your parents and siblings instead of immersing yourself in your own little digital world. Research says conversations and connections made at mealtimes can lead to your long-term success in life.[6]

3. Bedrooms. According to a large national survey, 43 percent of teens in the United States reported sleeping less than seven hours a night.[7] That number increased 22 percent from 2012 to 2015. What caused this alarming rise of sleep deprivation? One word: smartphones.

Sleep experts say you need at least nine hours of sleep per night. A lack of sleep can hurt school performance, add to anxiety and depression, and even contribute to acne and other skin problems. Less sleep also leads to poor decisions. Privacy and a lack of accountability do so as well. With the privacy of a bedroom and internet pornography a click away, it's not surprising that pornography addiction is on the rise. Honestly, one of the most mature and wisest decisions you can make is keeping digital devices out of your bedroom.

4. Vacations. Going away as a family is one of the best opportunities for deep relationship building. Don't let your devices get in the way.

Is it easy to take breaks from technology? No. In this Information Age it's easy to get addicted to tech. So, it will take time and effort. But the payoff can be huge. Instead of letting technology shape you, you'll take the lead in controlling your technology. And we all need help with this, so get some. Talk with your parents, youth leader, or close friend about helping you set boundaries and limits and checking in periodically to see how you're doing.

Speaking of your parents, share your passwords with them. Sounds outrageous, huh? Some students would rather face a zombie apocalypse than give out their passwords. But no matter your age, we all need accountability. And to be accountable, you must be transparent. When you live your online life with nothing to hide, you'll experience true freedom. If your parents haven't asked you for your passwords, voluntarily give them the information. Then smile at their shocked expressions as you explain your desire to control your online life and honor God in every single area of your life.

Part Three

Our Guide to Culture

It's time to get practical. In part 3, we tackle eight cultural challenges head-on. Every one of these can pound away at you like powerful waves. Each chapter is divided into four sections.

In the first section, "Don't Buy the Cultural Lies," false narratives of the culture will be exposed. Unless you're aware of them, cultural lies will undermine God's truth. Therefore, Jesus followers have an obligation to "destroy arguments and every lofty opinion raised against the knowledge of God" (2 Cor. 10:5).

The second section, "Recapture the Wonder of God's Story," explores the deep truths found in God's Story. As Christians, we should return to Scripture as our primary source for the knowledge of reality. In this section, each topic will be illuminated with relevant ideas and passages from God's Word.

"Action Steps," the third section, is designed to help you make biblical truth really practical. You can start with one or two suggestions and move on from there. Progress is your goal, not perfection.

The fourth section, "Hopecasting," will remind you that there is hope all around you, as God's Story continues to unfold from generation to generation.

Chapter Seven

Pornography

"There is no dignity when the human dimension is eliminated from the person. In short, the problem with pornography is not that it shows too much of the person, but that it shows far too little."
Pope John Paul II, *The Theology of the Body*

What would bother you more?

a. Looking at porn.

b. Throwing your plastic water bottle into the trash instead of the recycling bin.

The majority of students say it's *more immoral* to not recycle than it is to view porn.[1] Ninety percent of teens and 96 percent of young adults are either encouraging, accepting, or neutral when they talk about porn with their friends.[2] Because our culture largely views porn as harmless, too many are watching it.

- 49 percent of young adults say all or most of their friends use porn regularly.
- 41 percent of practicing Christian boys 13 to 24 use porn at least once a month.
- 23 percent of practicing Christian men 25+ use porn at least once a month.[3]
- One out of every eight online searches and one out of every five mobile searches is for porn.

- Pornography takes up one-third of the internet's bandwidth.[4]

Porn isn't confined to a particular gender, ethnicity, or socioeconomic status. It has no demographic or geographic barriers. It's just one click away. Many students seek it out, but even if you're not looking for porn, porn is looking for you. We're in the midst of a porn epidemic.

Maybe you're struggling with porn and wish you weren't, and it feels a little hopeless. It's not. As we wade into this difficult topic, remember, hope is always found in the gospel of Jesus Christ. Always.

Don't Buy the Cultural Lies

Lie #1: Porn is a harmless expression of human sexuality.
What is your friends' attitude toward porn? Are they pretty casual about it? How about you? Only one in ten teenagers report that their friends think watching porn is bad. Pornography, people might say, is just another way to express themselves sexually. Nobody is getting hurt, right? Add in the fact that you're used to having immediate access to whatever you're looking for, and it's a recipe for disaster.

You need to know that porn *is* addictive. In the groundbreaking book *Hooked: New Science on How Casual Sex Is Affecting Our Children*, two doctors demonstrated how chemicals released in the brain during sexual activity can lead to addiction.[5] Being addicted to pornography actually changes the structure of your brain in ways similar to being addicted to drugs and alcohol.

Porn also has serious personal consequences. Viewing porn distorts our attitudes about sexuality, leading to greater sexual promiscuity and risky sexual behavior. Later in life, it will affect your marriage by decreasing satisfaction and breaking down trust with your spouse. In the end, people are left with perpetual feelings of shame and guilt.[6]

Lie #2: Porn is personal; it's no one's business.

The effects of porn aren't limited to the person watching. Have you thought about how dehumanizing porn is? It treats people as objects for the gratification of others. As a result, the porn industry is littered with broken lives. According to researcher Dr. Mary Anne Layden:

> Once [the pornography actresses] are in the industry they have high rates of substance abuse, typically alcohol and cocaine, depression, borderline personality disorder … The experience I find most common among the performers is that they have to be drunk, high or dissociated in order to go to work. Their work environment is particularly toxic.… The terrible work life of the pornography performer is often followed by an equally terrible home life. They have an increased risk of sexually transmitted disease including HIV, domestic violence and have about a 25% chance of making a marriage that lasts as long as 3 years.[7]

There are a number of other social costs as well. Porn fuels sex trafficking and leads to increased violence and exploitation of women and children. It also breaks apart marriages and families.

But do we really need statistics? Common sense tells us that porn is poisonous. Pornography kills sexual intimacy. It kills relationships. And it kills our spiritual lives. Porn only brings destruction.

Recapture the Wonder of God's Story

If we want to know what humanity is designed *for*, we must know the One who designed it. If we have questions about the way we ought to live, we must consult the Designer. In particular, we need to refer to His design manual: Scripture.

God's Story—the true Story about all of reality—begins with Genesis 1:1 when "God created the heavens and the earth." Humanity isn't the end product of a purposeless collision of atoms. We are fashioned by the Grand Designer. Our body and soul are constructed carefully and purposefully. Human beings are "fearfully and wonderfully made" (Ps. 139:14) and meant to be in relationship with God and one another. Therefore, we must follow His design for human relationships if we want to thrive.

Sexuality was intended to be experienced in a one-flesh union between husband and wife—not in isolation. "Therefore a man shall leave his father and his mother and hold fast to his wife, and they shall become one flesh. And the man and his wife were both naked and were not ashamed" (Gen. 2:24–25). There is no shame in God's design for sexuality—only beauty and delight.

Scripture never endorses sexuality in isolation. Not once. But porn takes the relational context out of sexuality. It disconnects sex from a relationship between two people who love each other and deforms it into a means for personal indulgence. Watching porn is a thoroughly selfish pursuit.

In addition, Jesus is clear about His feelings on lust: "You have heard that it was said, 'You shall not commit adultery.' But I say to you that everyone who looks at a woman with lustful intent has already committed adultery with her in his heart" (Matt. 5:27–28). To look at another person lustfully—pornography's main objective—violates God's design and carries severe consequences.

Adultery of body or heart sets us on a trajectory of disgrace and destruction. Listen carefully to this warning from Proverbs 6:

> Do not desire her beauty in your heart,
>> and do not let her capture you with her eyelashes;
> for the price of a prostitute is only a loaf of bread,
>> but a married woman hunts down a precious life.
> Can a man carry fire next to his chest

and his clothes not be burned?
Or can one walk on hot coals
and his feet not be scorched?

So is God against sex? No! The Song of Solomon is a divinely inspired book that reveals God's wonderful intentions for human sexuality in the context of marriage. In contrast to culture's lustful passions and uncontrolled sexual desire, God's Story paints a breathtaking picture of the beauty and intimacy of sex within marriage.

Action Steps

Knowing the truth about porn and God's design for sexuality is only half the battle. We must also act. The following steps are designed to make biblical truth practical. Don't be overwhelmed by the following list, thinking you have to take on every step immediately. Just be open to them, start with one or two suggestions at first, and as you make progress, add more action steps.

1. Wake up! Open your eyes to the breadth and depth of the consequences of porn. Visit the National Center on Sexual Exploitation's website (www.endsexualexploitation.org), and download the free ebook *Pornography: A Public Health Crisis*. Open your eyes to the destructive effects of porn and acknowledge what it is—porn is sin and the porn industry is evil. Knowing the truth will help motivate you to take action.

2. Confront the problem. Do you have your own battle with porn? Do you have a friend who is struggling with porn addiction but never had a conversation with him or her about it? This is a battle and we need others who will fight it with us, side by side. Confess your porn habits to God and to one another—such as your parents, a trustworthy friend, or your youth pastor. Get accountability. You may need to seek the help of a professional

Christian counselor to begin repairing the damage porn has caused in your life. Let the grace of the gospel wash over you as you experience God's forgiveness. Let the Holy Spirit sanctify you by His power as He begins the process of removing this sin from your life.

3. Protect yourself. Did you know the average age of exposure to porn is eleven? If you haven't seen porn yet, do something now to inject some major accountability in your life. Prevention is better than recovery.

Talk with your parents about buying and installing internet filters that block pornographic content. Access should be filtered on every device in your home, including desktop computers, laptops, tablets, smartphones, and gaming consoles. Finally, speak with your parents about enabling restrictions on your internet browsing devices (under "Settings"). It may be difficult to give up this kind of freedom, but when our freedom leads to overwhelming temptation and destructive sin, we have to make sacrifices.

It may shock your parents (in a good way) when you initiate this conversation. But remember: when you choose to protect yourself, you'll honor God and strengthen your relationship with Him and others.

4. Be honest about the consequences of viewing porn. Do a Google search on the "negative effects of pornography." You'll find research demonstrating porn's ability to rewire the brain and create addicts, especially at young ages. You'll discover data that links porn with social anxiety, depression, low motivation, lack of productivity, and feelings of guilt and shame. You'll see porn's harmful effects on marriages: how it decreases interest in sex with one's spouse and increases divorce among the addicted. And the list goes on.

5. Understand the darkness of the porn industry. The apostle Paul warns to "take no part in the unfruitful works of darkness, but instead expose them" (Eph. 5:11). Being honest about the porn industry helps it lose some of its attraction. Don't fool yourself into thinking everyone involved is a willing participant. It's an industry filled with sexually transmitted diseases (STDs), prostitution, drug abuse, emotional manipulation, violence, and even the exploitation of women and children for sex trafficking.

6. Build strong relationships. No internet filter or monitoring system can replace loving relationships. The best defense against pornography is a close family. So spend time with the people you love and who love you. Make time for your mom, dad, siblings, church friends, or leaders. And worship together. Work hard to find a solid local church or youth group, and then plug in. The body of Christ is essential to your spiritual growth.

7. Be ready to forgive yourself and seek God's grace. In a world where porn is normal and readily available, if you've seen it, you're not alone. That's the bad news. The good news is that you can experience forgiveness through Christ's sacrifice on the cross. The apostle Paul wrote, "There is therefore now no condemnation for those who are in Christ Jesus. For the law of the Spirit of life has set you free in Christ Jesus from the law of sin and death" (Rom. 8:1–2). Only Christ can offer you freedom from addiction and hope amid guilt and shame. Only Christ can restore your willpower to resist sin and temptation. Don't let the shame of porn short-circuit your relationship with Christ. Go to Him, confess your sin, and ask Him to help you walk the path to true freedom.

Hopecasting

Although we started with the destructive consequences of porn, there are hopeful signs the tide could be turning. In 2015, the worldwide Hilton hotel chain—with 540 properties in more than eighty countries—announced that it would remove porn channels from all of its hotels.[8] This was in response to a three-year public campaign spearheaded by the National Center on Sexual Exploitation.

Celebrities are speaking out against pornography. English comedian and actor Russell Brand posted a YouTube video warning about the damaging effects of porn on relationships.[9] Former NFL player-turned-actor Terry Crews posted a series of Facebook videos titled *Dirty Little Secret*, in which he confessed his own porn addiction and acknowledged his need for professional help.[10] Now he campaigns against the dangers of porn.

Even former *Playboy* model Pamela Anderson is weighing in. In an unlikely partnership, she and a Jewish rabbi coauthored an op-ed article in the *Wall Street Journal* titled "Take the Pledge: No More Indulging Porn." The piece warns of pornography's "corrosive effect on a man's soul."[11] If even a former *Playboy* centerfold sees the need to issue such a serious warning, then there's hope for change!

The porn culture and its appeal may seem unstoppable. It will take a seismic shift in the attitudes of society if it's going to be conquered. Young Christians can help lead the culture out of the darkness of sexual sin and into the light of Christ. It can start with hope and healing in your own life and in the lives of your friends.

Chapter Eight

The Hookup Culture

"[God] doesn't ask us not to have sex because He wants rules and stuff. He's like "I'm trying to protect you from hurt and pain." I think sex can cause a lot of pain. Sometimes people have sex because they don't feel good enough, because they lack self-worth. Women do that, and guys do that."

Justin Bieber, explaining why he abstained from sex after having
a "legitimate problem with sex" (February 2019 *Vogue*)

Sade Patterson, a student at the University of New Mexico, watched for two years as her school hosted its annual Sex Week. This student-led event was supposed to "educate" students on all things sexual. Workshops included "How to Be a Gentlemen and Still Get Laid" and "How to Have Threesomes." "Educators" like Dirty Lola (an advocate of sadomasochism) were invited to teach. After listening to presentations containing all kinds of falsehoods,[1] Patterson decided to do something.

Through her Students for Life campus club, she put together an alternative event called the Real Sex Week. Instead of crude content and a focus on self-gratification, the event provided students with beneficial sex education. Workshops dealt with topics like the impact of sex on students' minds and relationships, the negative effects of abortion, support for pregnant and parenting students, the biology behind intercourse, and the benefits of waiting for sex until marriage. She definitely got pushback, but Patterson reported strong attendance at the event.[2]

Thankfully, Sade Patterson didn't buy into culture's lies about sex. Will you?

Don't Buy the Cultural Lies

You're surrounded by a hookup culture that says sex with no strings attached is perfectly normal. Everybody's doing it. Besides, what's wrong with a little sexual experimentation before you get into a serious relationship? Marriage is a long way off, so who's really going to wait?

Lie #1: Everyone is hooking up.

Not everyone is doing it. In fact, the hookup trend seems to be heading downward. A recent study in the *Archives of Sexual Behavior* demonstrated that millennials are twice as likely to be sexually *inactive* than previous generations.[3] In the study, millennials reported fewer sex partners than any group since the 1960s. The number of high school students who reported having sex fell to 30 percent in 2015 from 34 percent in 2013 and 37.5 percent in 1991.[4]

Lie #2: Hooking up is consequence-free.

First, hookups increase the risk of sexually transmitted diseases. According to the Centers for Disease Control and Prevention, sexually transmitted diseases like chlamydia, gonorrhea, and syphilis are on the rise, especially for young people. The "CDC estimates that nearly 20 million new sexually transmitted infections occur every year in this country, half among young people aged 15–24."[5] Chlamydia can cause permanent damage to a woman's reproductive system, even leading to infertility. Some types of the human papillomavirus (HPV), the most common sexually transmitted infection, can cause head and neck cancer, cervical cancer, and genital warts. Worse yet, there is no treatment for HPV.[6]

Second, hookup behavior during college is correlated with depression and poor mental health.[7] Ohio State University surveyed approximately ten thousand young people about their romantic relationships and found that teens who experienced depression were more likely to have casual sex as young adults.[8]

Third, hooking up is associated with other risky behaviors. According to the *Journal of Sex Research*, 53 percent of women drank during hook-ups—and 38 percent drank heavily. The less they knew their hookup partner, the more likely they were to drink, and drink heavily, before sex.[9]

Lie #3: What you do when you're young won't impact your future.
Hooking up now will undermine your marriage later. Eighty percent of students see marriage as an important part of their life plans.[10] However, permissive sexual behavior sabotages marital stability. Individuals with more sex partners before marriage report less marital satisfaction. On the other hand, having fewer sexual partners results in higher marital quality.[11]

Today's so-called sexual freedom insists that all consensual sex acts are good. But clearly, casual sex delivers brokenness.

Recapture the Wonder of God's Story

For too long, the church's main contribution to the cultural conversation on sex has been to shout: "Don't do it!" But God's Story offers so much more than just a simple no to premarital sex. For every prohibition, there is a beautiful, life-giving yes!

God's Story begins with God as creator and designer. Human design and identity are grounded in His nature. Questions like "Who am I?" "What am I?" and "How do I function properly?" find their proper starting point in God's existence and creative activity.

Built into God's design for humanity is a union between a man and a woman within the husband-wife context: "A man shall leave his father and his mother and hold fast to his wife, and they shall become one flesh" (Gen. 2:24). God's plan is one man and one woman, becoming one flesh, for a lifetime. The sexual desire men and women have for each other is a good thing that God designed, so it makes sense that we look to Him for vision, guidance, and wisdom in this area.

It may surprise you, but first and foremost, God's primary purpose for sex isn't personal pleasure. That's right, sex is for making babies. God's first command to Adam and Eve was to "be fruitful and multiply and fill the earth" (Gen. 1:28). Therefore, sex shouldn't be completely severed from reproduction. Why? Because our creator fashioned family for a permanent commitment between husband and wife to be the proper and ideal environment for childbearing and, thus, filling the earth.

But second, sex is pleasurable. Sexual desire isn't a problem. Disordered sexual desire is. God says yes to sexuality between husband and wife but no to lust. Sex *is* good, and that's why it must be protected and cultivated. Consider Proverbs 5:18–19:

> Let your fountain be blessed,
>> and rejoice in the wife of your youth,
>> a lovely deer, a graceful doe.
> Let her breasts fill you at all times with delight;
>> be intoxicated always in her love.

Yes, those verses are in the inspired Word of God.

Think about it. Only an amazing God could think up something so beautiful and wonderful and thrilling as sex, which also serves His purpose of populating the world.

God's design brings together pleasure and purpose. Sexuality is God's gift, and His gifts are good: "For everything created by God is good" (1 Tim. 4:4). In contrast, our culture says that sex is merely a means to our personal satisfaction.

God's Story makes it clear that the gift of sexuality belongs only within the context of a husband-wife marriage (1 Cor. 7:2). Why? First, the exclusivity and commitment of marriage is the best environment to care for the product of sex: children. Second, marriage cultivates the love, safety, security, and trust needed for sexual intimacy to flourish.

The hookup culture is powerless to deliver both love and intimacy. God's Word contains His design for sexuality contrasted with the ugly consequences of illicit sexual activity. Yes, we are the pinnacle of God's creation, but we're also fallen, sinful creatures. We are beautiful *and* broken. Dignified yet depraved. For this reason, Scripture offers strong warnings:

- **Say no to sexual immorality:** "For this is the will of God, your sanctification: that you abstain from sexual immorality; that each one of you know how to control his own body in holiness and honor" (1 Thess. 4:3–4).
- **Say no to lust:** "Everyone who looks at a woman with lustful intent has already committed adultery with her in his heart" (Matt. 5:28).
- **Say no to adultery:** "Let marriage be held in honor among all, and let the marriage bed be undefiled, for God will judge the sexually immoral and adulterous" (Heb. 13:4).

God's "no" commands—His moral rules—are meant to protect you. The hookup culture is a cheap imitation of real love. It results in pain, suffering, regret, and shame. Recapture the wonder of God's Story about sexuality. Not only is it better; it's beautiful.

Action Steps

1. Look to your parents for guidance on sex. Culture bombards you with bad messages about sex. Seek knowledge and wisdom by talking with your parents. Yes, the first conversation may be awkward, but keep talking. In fact, do not just have "the talk"; make it an ongoing conversation. Ask them their views on sex and marriage, what mistakes they made, and how you can avoid them. Share with them your own struggles and the pressures you face.

2. Understand the yes as well as the no. If you only think about what you're not supposed to do, you'll probably start with the wrong questions, like "How far is too far?" Sexual purity isn't a line to avoid crossing; it's a direction of life that moves toward marriage. Remind yourself of God's beautiful picture of sexuality within the safety and intimacy of marriage.

3. Seek healthy dating relationships. As you find yourself attracted to someone, remember the connection of dating to marriage. This can be difficult when your emotions (and hormones) are off the charts, so there's wisdom in waiting to date. Once you start to date, be wise about the situations you put yourself in. Here are some good boundaries to consider in your dating relationships:

- *Only date Christians.* If dating is a first step toward marriage, it's unwise to date someone who doesn't share your faith in Christ. That's why God warns us against it (2 Cor. 6:14; 1 Cor. 7:39).
- *Never be alone with a date.* Isolation often encourages sexual temptation. Staying in public creates accountability.
- *Stick to a reasonable curfew.* Not much good happens when you're out late.
- *Go in a group.* Every date doesn't have to be a group date, but having other couples around helps take off some of the pressure.
- *Don't date exclusively during high school.* Avoiding exclusivity keeps you from getting serious too quickly.
- *Listen to Mom and Dad.* As parents, they have the experience to spot unhealthy relationships and unwise plans. And because they care so much about you, they can provide godly advice.

4. Be a gentleman. This one's just for the guys. Take the lead in a dating relationship. That means asking a girl out, going to the front door, meeting the parents, planning the date, paying for the meal (and praying before it), and general manners. Don't settle for the low expectations of our culture. Raise the bar and treat your date with respect. She's more than a date; she's an image bearer of God! If she's a Christian, she's also your sister in Christ.

5. Be a lady. This one's just for the girls. Expect your date to treat you with respect. If he's not coming to the door to pick you up, don't go out. Hold to what you know God says about your identity and be confident. Be honest enough to treat the guys you're dating with respect. They're God's children too.

6. Pray and trust God. Maybe you already carry scars from your own sexual sin. Or maybe your parents haven't provided healthy dialogue and direction on this topic. Lay down your fears and failures at God's feet and put your trust in Him. It's never too late to rebuild healthy relationships. Remember, the power of God is greater than the power of our sexualized culture.

Hopecasting

So what hope is there when you're surrounded by a sexually promiscuous culture? Remember, God's truth about sexuality is true and good and beautiful. Even if you've made mistakes in the past or are currently in an unhealthy sexual relationship, God rescues, forgives, provides wisdom, and will help you build a healthy future.

During a Q-and-A session at a high school summer camp in California, a girl approached the microphone and asked the speaker, "My friend wants to know if you're in a sexually active Christian relationship that is healthy and not dependent on or defined by sex, can you be 100 percent committed to Christ, given that you've prayed about the situation and act out of love and not lust?"

The speaker thought for a moment and then pointed out that the only healthy sexually active relationship is between a husband and wife. The Scriptures clearly teach that. Two unmarried high schoolers having sex is unhealthy by definition. After he answered the question, she sat down and another female student approached the microphone.

"That was actually *my* question," she admitted. "I've been in this relationship for over a year now. My boyfriend and I prayed about it for about ten months and came to this decision. So am I not 100 percent committed to Christ?"

Although he felt grace and compassion for this girl, the speaker had to respond with God's truth. "This is actually a decision you didn't need to pray about," he said. "God has already spoken, and sex between a boyfriend and girlfriend is sin. If you thought you heard God say this is okay, that was not God."

Tears began to stream down her cheeks. She quickly left the microphone and returned to her seat.

Seeing her pain, the speaker added, "I don't say this out of anger but out of love. I love you students like my younger brothers and sisters, so that's why I am compelled to speak the truth to you. Premarital sex will harm you, it will harm your relationship with your boyfriend, and it will harm your relationship with God."

Later, the speaker learned that this high schooler called her boyfriend and broke off their relationship. She had heard God's truth, the Lord opened her eyes, she repented of her sin, and she responded in obedience. Yes, she experienced temporary pain and heartbreak. But she was now on the path of redemption and restoration.

Without question, Christ followers must broadcast Jesus' offer of grace, forgiveness, and redemption to a sexually bankrupt culture. We must also offer God's vision for human sexuality as a beautiful and achievable goal.

Chapter Nine

Sexual Orientation

"How do we make an identity out of temptation? By collapsing what you desire with who you are. By collapsing what tempts you or what trips you up with who you will become.... God's revealed purpose for my identity always nails me to His cross."

Rosaria Butterfield, *Openness Unhindered*

Rosaria Butterfield was a lesbian college professor of English and women's studies at Syracuse University. She was an outspoken activist in the LGBTQ community, living happily with her partner. And she despised Christians.

Then she met pastor Ken Smith and his wife, Floy. Unexpectedly, they became friends. The Smiths invited Rosaria into their home to share meals and thoughtful conversation. Rosaria returned the favor, and the Smiths were happy to enter her world as well. Because Pastor Ken and his wife were kind, hospitable, and welcoming, Rosaria felt safe with them.

After two years of genuine friendship with the Smiths—in which she was able to ask honest questions and wrestle with the claims of the Bible—Rosaria Butterfield put her trust in Jesus and eventually walked away from her lesbian lifestyle. Now she's the wife of a pastor and a mother of four children.[1]

These are the stories our culture does *not* want you to hear.

Instead, when it comes to LGBTQ issues, Christians are portrayed as hate-filled bigots. But do Ken and Floy Smith sound like hateful people?

They showed nothing but love and kindness to Rosaria Butterfield. Today, however, that's not nearly enough. Culture won't tolerate someone who doesn't hold the "right" view on this issue, which is complete acceptance and affirmation of the gay lifestyle.

The cultural momentum is ready to silence the church with this issue. In fact, Christians have already been punished for their views on gay and lesbian relationships, from losing their jobs and being forced to close businesses to being fined large sums of money by state commissions. So how should followers of Christ move forward? Should we abandon the view that the church has held consistently for the last two thousand years? No, we must always be faithful to the way of Jesus.

Jesus was "full of grace and truth" (John 1:14), and He is the model for our engagement on all issues. Therefore, we must first think carefully about the intellectual issues surrounding sexual orientation. Then, like Ken and Floy Smith, the truth should cause us to walk with our gay family and friends in love, kindness, and compassion.

Don't Buy the Cultural Lies

Lie #1: Christians treat gays and lesbians terribly.

At a student outreach event, I (Brett) was approached by a teenager who sincerely loved his gay friends but was bothered by his perception of the church's treatment of gays and lesbians.

"You've grown up and have been active in the church, right?" I asked.

The student nodded.

"So that means you've seen the way Christians speak and act almost every week for the last sixteen years of your life," I continued.

The teen nodded again.

"In those sixteen years, how many times did you personally witness a Christian treating a gay person terribly?" I asked.

The student thought for a moment. "Actually, I've never seen it myself," he finally answered.

Think about that. He had grown up in the church and had a very negative perception of Christians' actions toward the homosexual community but had never personally observed such mistreatment.

The truth is, all people—gay or straight—are God's image bearers and should be treated with dignity and respect. And the clear evidence from the lives of actual Christians shows that the vast majority of Christians treat their gay friends with nothing but kindness.

However, the cultural perception among non-Christians, and even some Christians, is that the church hates people living a gay lifestyle. This impression comes from a media-saturated culture that constantly posts images of picketing fringe "Christian" groups like Westboro Baptist Church or distorts news stories of people wanting to hold to their own beliefs in an effort to characterize all Christians. The actions of Westboro Baptist Church are utterly deplorable. They don't reflect Jesus and the truth of the Bible.

The reality is most Christians do not mistreat gay people. Christians want to share what the entire world, including the gay community, desperately needs: the forgiveness and restoration that only Jesus can offer.

Understanding the existence of these falsehoods is important because they build a barrier between the gay community and the Christian community. If the gay community perceives the church to be full of judgment and hatred, it will shun us—which it has. We should instead seek to build relationships with generous, loving action that will help others come to know Jesus.

Lie #2: Gay people are born that way.
From Lady Gaga's album *Born This Way* to television sitcoms and movies, pop culture repeats over and over: Same-sex attraction is innate. Therefore, we're told, homosexual behavior is a legitimate form of sexual expression.

First, an action or disposition isn't morally justified simply because it has genetic origins. For example, if researchers discovered genes that contribute to alcoholism or violent behavior, would that justify drunkenness or murder? Even if a gay gene is discovered, the moral question of homosexual activity would still be unsettled.

Second, there is no compelling scientific study proving homosexuality is biologically determined.[2] There is evidence, however, against this claim. Studies of twins undermine the claim that a gay gene exists. Since identical twins share identical genetics, whenever there is one gay twin, it would follow that the other twin should be gay as well a large percent of the time. However, researchers found that in cases where one twin is gay, the other twin is also gay less than 15 percent of the time.[3]

The American Psychological Association (APA) also recognizes the lack of scientific evidence for the claim that homosexuality is genetic: "Although much research has examined the possible genetic, hormonal, developmental, social and cultural influences on sexual orientation, no findings have emerged that permit scientists to conclude that sexual orientation is determined by any particular factor or factors."[4]

Third, the fact there is an ex-gay community clearly contradicts the born-this-way theory. Men and women whose same-sex attractions have changed don't fit the gay-gene narrative. Their stories are rarely told, but there are thousands of ex-gay men and women who now live heterosexual or celibate lifesyles.[5]

So if people aren't born gay, is there another explanation? Many suggest gay people choose their same-sex attractions. Here it's helpful to distinguish between action and attraction. Gay men and women certainly choose the behavior they engage in and are responsible for their actions. Just as heterosexuals don't choose their attractions, homosexuals find themselves with attractions and often report them as unwanted.

Instead of thinking of sexual orientation as either innate or chosen, a third explanation may provide the best explanation. There is strong evidence that both developmental and environmental factors play a prominent role in forming a same-sex attraction between birth and young adulthood.[6]

Lie #3: The gay lifestyle is just as normal and healthy as heterosexuality.
When you pull back the curtain on the gay lifestyle, this claim is clearly
false. First, monogamy is almost nonexistent in homosexual relationships.
Only 4.5 percent of homosexual men in current relationships report being
faithful to their partners. In contrast, 75 percent of heterosexual men and
85 percent of women report being faithful to their spouses.[7] Promiscuity
among lesbians is high as well.[8]

Second, homosexual behavior greatly increases the risk of sexually
transmitted diseases like HIV, chlamydia, gonorrhea, and syphilis. Men
who have sex with men have by far the highest rate of syphilis infections
(83 percent) among men.[9] Gay and bisexual men are at greater risk for
HIV infection than any other group in the United States. They make up
approximately 2 percent of the population but account for 55 percent of
the HIV infections.[10]

Third, gay men and women are more likely to experience emotional,
psychological, and physical harm. The CDC found the following to be
more prevalent among gay, lesbian, and bisexual students than heterosexual students:

- Physical dating violence (17.5 percent compared to
  8.3 percent)
- Sexual dating violence (22.7 percent compared to 9.1
  percent)
- Feelings of sadness or hopelessness (60.4 percent compared to 26.4 percent)[11]

Many in our culture dismiss the high numbers of psychological
disorders and substance abuse or claim these problems are the result of discrimination and poor treatment of the gay community. However, even in
gay-friendly countries like the Netherlands, where same-sex marriage has
been legal since 2001, rates of anxiety, depression, and drug dependence
are much higher among gay men and women.[12]

This data isn't meant to make gay family members and friends look bad. Because the lives and well-being of people are at stake, we need to take an honest and sobering look at the facts before we affirm a lifestyle that causes great harm. As Christians, we should also be moved to love and show compassion for people we know who live a gay lifestyle.

Recapture the Wonder of God's Story

At the heart of every sexual issue is the question of identity. Sexual orientation is a prime example. When asked about marriage and divorce, Jesus answers by taking us back to the beginning of creation:

> Have you not read that he who created them from the beginning made them male and female, and said, "Therefore a man shall leave his father and his mother and hold fast to his wife, and the two shall become one flesh"? So they are no longer two but one flesh. What therefore God has joined together, let not man separate. (Matt. 19:4–6)

God's Story doesn't start with "Thou shalt not" but with "God saw that it was good" (Gen. 1:10). The primary emphasis of His Word is not homosexuality and its sinfulness. Instead Jesus calls attention to the way He designed males and females to become husband and wife. This one-flesh union is God's true, good, and beautiful plan for humanity. Men and women were designed for each other. This union alone achieves God's purpose to "be fruitful and multiply and fill the earth" (v. 28).

In light of God's design, there are significant implications for the gay lifestyle. First, homosexuality violates God's creational norms. Men and women weren't designed to engage sexually with a partner of the same sex. That's why the apostle Paul described gay and lesbian behavior as exchanging "the natural function for that which is unnatural" (Rom. 1:26 NASB).

Homosexual behavior is unnatural because it disregards God's natural order of creation.

Second, homosexual behavior is sin. Romans 1:24–28 makes the clearest pronouncement in all of Scripture on the subject:

> Therefore God gave [people] over in the lusts of their hearts to impurity, so that their bodies would be dishonored among them. For they exchanged the truth of God for a lie, and worshiped and served the creature rather than the Creator, who is blessed forever. Amen.
>
> For this reason God gave them over to degrading passions; for their women exchanged the natural function for that which is unnatural, and in the same way also the men abandoned the natural function of the woman and burned in their desire toward one another, men with men committing indecent acts and receiving in their own persons the due penalty of their error.
>
> And just as they did not see fit to acknowledge God any longer, God gave them over to a depraved mind, to do those things which are not proper. (NASB)

Homosexuality is addressed elsewhere in Scripture as well (e.g., Lev. 18:22; 20:13; 1 Cor. 6:9–10; 1 Tim. 1:8–11). Sin is the violation of God's moral law. Just like all other sinners, gay men and women aren't victims of their biology; they act in their own free will and are responsible for their choices.

Third, homosexuality attempts to replace God-given identity with self-identity. We don't answer to God; we answer only to ourselves. Even our identity becomes what we make it. Think about the statements "I'm gay" or "I'm a lesbian." For the first time in human history, people are defining themselves in terms of their sexual desires. Over fifty gender options are offered on Facebook, and many institutions, including workplaces and universities, insist that you respect the pronouns people choose for themselves.[13]

No matter how much we attempt to redefine our reality, it will only serve to run us head-on into God's reality. The apostle Paul strongly warned,

> Do not be deceived: neither the sexually immoral, nor idolaters, nor adulterers, nor men who practice homosexuality, nor thieves, nor the greedy, nor drunkards, nor revilers, nor swindlers will inherit the kingdom of God. (1 Cor. 6:9–10)

Thank God for the good news of the gospel. Immediately following these verses, Paul declared, "And such were some of you. But you were washed, you were sanctified, you were justified in the name of the Lord Jesus Christ and by the Spirit of our God" (v. 11). God's forgiveness and healing are available to all—no matter our lifestyle choices. Not only does God's Story describe our fall into sin; it also proclaims our redemption by His grace.

Action Steps

1. Acknowledge that sexual brokenness isn't confined to homosexual behavior. Other kinds of sexual sin—premarital sex and pornography—are much more common and also wrong. As G. K. Chesterton once said, "There are many ways to fall down, but only one way to stand up straight."

2. Resist culture's false view of love. Culture tries to tell us that love equals full acceptance, that if you truly love your gay friends and family members, you'll embrace them on their terms. That means being tolerant—treating people with respect even while you disagree with their beliefs or behavior—is not enough. But true love doesn't require accepting everything someone says or does. Clearly, parents love their children without affirming their harmful actions. In the same way, Jesus always loved without compromising the truth. (For example, see Jesus' interaction with the woman at the well in John 4:1–30.) Loving people often requires telling them the truth, even if they don't want to hear it. You can't control their response.

3. Don't shun gay family members and friends. The apostle Paul made it clear that we aren't to dissociate ourselves from "the sexually immoral of this world … since then you would need to go out of the world" (1 Cor. 5:9–10). Of course, it's a different story regarding sexually immoral believers (vv. 11–13). Loving people in a broken world can get messy, so also remember to pray for your gay friends.

4. Make Jesus, not homosexuality, the main issue. The most important thing about us isn't what we believe about homosexuality but what we do with the claims of Christ. Therefore, the priority is pointing your non-Christian gay friends to Christ for salvation, not converting them to heterosexuality. Once they put their trust in Jesus, God's Spirit will help them find their true identity, as a new creation in Christ.

5. Prepare for the social costs of affirming biblical views. The days of socially acceptable Christianity are over. Christians are now mocked, ostracized, and punished for merely holding biblical views on homosexuality. It will happen today, just as it happened in Jesus' time. In John 15:18–20, Jesus said:

> If the world hates you, know that it has hated me before it hated you. If you were of the world, the world would love you as its own; but because you are not of the world, but I chose you out of the world, therefore the world hates you. Remember the word that I said to you: "A servant is not greater than his master." If they persecuted me, they will also persecute you.

Hopecasting

No matter how far the culture strays from the truth on this issue, there is always the hope of redemption in Jesus Christ. Beautiful, real-life stories remind us of this.

Christopher Yuan, the son of Chinese immigrants, never fit in with his American classmates when he was growing up. Early exposure to pornography awakened his same-sex attractions. While attending dental school, he started down a path to homosexuality. After Yuan came out to his family, he slowly descended into a fast-paced gay lifestyle, as well as doing and dealing drugs. He was eventually arrested and sentenced to prison. During his incarceration, he discovered he was HIV positive. Through the prayers of his parents, who had become Christians, and reading God's Word (he'd pulled a Gideon Bible from a prison garbage can), Christopher Yuan gave his life to Christ. He now teaches at Moody Bible Institute and has a worldwide speaking ministry.[14]

Hope and healing are always possible in God's Story. Jesus is reconciling gay and straight sinners to the Father. His desire is to restore everyone to new life through the power of His resurrection.

Chapter Ten

Gender Identity

"'Sex change' is biologically impossible. People who undergo sex-reassignment surgery do not change from men to women or vice versa. Rather, they become feminized men or masculinized women."

Dr. Paul McHugh, "Transgender Surgery Isn't the Solution"

In our culture, the words *male* and *female* are outdated. These terms assume a fixed gender binary. And everyone knows you can't assume a person's gender anymore, right? So the culture has created a new word, *cisgender*, to refer to individuals "who have a gender identity that matches the sex that they were assigned at birth."[1]

But that definition raises questions: Assigned by whom? Parents, medical professionals, society, the individual? Make no mistake, new words and new definitions are not always neutral or harmless. The term *cisgender* has two assumptions built right into the definition. First, that sex is "assigned" and not a biological reality. And second, that gender is chosen, not innate. And even though many in our culture buy into these assumptions, we shouldn't. A video that went viral on YouTube[2] illustrates some of the problems that result from today's confusion on gender identity.

Joseph Backholm, former president of the Family Policy Institute of Washington, asked students at the University of Washington about their views on gender identity and public-restroom policy. At first, the students affirmed the right of every individual to choose the bathroom that corresponds to their perceived gender. Backholm followed up with a series of questions:

- "If I told you that I was a woman, what would your response be?"
- "If I told you that I was Chinese, what would your response be?"
- "If I told you that I was seven years old, what would your response be?"
- "If I told you I'm six feet five inches, what would you say?"

Amazingly, the vast majority of students were unwilling to say that Backholm wasn't anything he claimed to be. One particular student's answer sums up the responses: "If you thoroughly debated me or explained why you felt that you were six foot five, I feel like I would be very open to saying that you were six foot five or Chinese or a woman."

However, Joseph Backholm is a five-foot-nine-inch white guy. In this brave new world, gender—and almost *anything* we believe about ourselves—is fluid.

Don't Buy the Cultural Lies

Lie #1: Gender is merely a social construction.

When it comes to gender and sexuality, our culture says there are no objective truths, only subjective preferences. If you feel it, declare it to the world, and it becomes so. Gender, we're told, is not rooted in biology; instead, it's what's referred to as a social construct, which just means an idea people within a culture create ("construct").

There is no dominant vision of gender identity for our culture, and no limit. And we're beginning to see the endless absurdities that follow from this reasoning. There are people who wear pet collars, eat from a bowl, and identify as dogs.[3] There are grown men who identify as little girls.[4] There are individuals who marry themselves (called *sologamy*).[5] If we can create our own gender identity, why can't we create *any* identity we want? Social construction is free to go anywhere our minds will take us.

But this slippery slope can't hold up under the weight of its own consequences. If you self-identify as a sixty-five-year-old man, should the federal government start sending you Social Security checks? If you self-identify as a six-year-old girl, should you be able to enroll in first-grade at the local public elementary school? If the answer is no, then why is a biological male who identifies as a female allowed to impact the laws of the land so that he can use the restroom or locker room of his choice?[6]

Lie #2: We should validate people's thoughts and desires so they'll flourish.

The culture encourages, "Be who you are." Whatever reality you select for yourself is just fine. In fact, the choice to defy reality is often viewed as an act of courage (as in the case of Bruce "Caitlyn" Jenner). Anyone who merely questions a person's view of their own reality is labeled a bigot. The definition of "tolerance" has shifted. We must now accept and affirm whatever lifestyle someone chooses. If a man thinks he is a woman in his own mind, he must be a woman in your mind also.

So how can we respond? First, it's not bigotry; it's biology. Objective facts about physiology, anatomy, chromosomes, and DNA exist. Maleness and femaleness are undeniable physical realities. On the other hand, there are no objective medical or scientific tests to determine transgenderism. It exists only in the mind of the individual. It's purely subjective.

Essentially, a doctor cannot diagnose an individual as transgender. The individual diagnoses him- or herself. Instead of treating someone's psychological confusion, the gender-identity movement says that sex-reassignment (or what is now being called gender-confirmation) surgery is the answer. But is it? If surgery were indeed a biological fix for gender-identity confusion, transgender people wouldn't regret their sex-change surgeries. Yet, a significant number do.[7]

A person may be able to alter his or her physical appearance, but reality remains. The empirical data demonstrates that sex-reassignment surgery isn't helping the transgender community. Many don't flourish after surgery; they continue to struggle. As difficult as it may be for transgender people to hear, psychological causes are the best explanation for gender confusion. Therefore, if we treat the body and *not* the mind, we won't be able to help our friends and family struggling with their gender identities.

Only in the case of transgenderism are physical solutions offered for a psychological incongruence, which are very permanent. For example, a ninety-pound teenage girl who struggles with anorexia may believe she is grossly overweight. But doctors won't do surgery to make her body thinner. They don't doubt her feelings, but they consider her self-perception inaccurate and therefore treat her mental and emotional health.

Recapture the Wonder of God's Story

You won't find the word *transgender* in Scripture, but that doesn't mean God has nothing to say about the issue. He speaks directly and explicitly about gender in the creation account: "Male and female [God] created them" (Gen. 1:27). God didn't make gender-neutral humans. Gender is part of God's design, deeply grounded in His created order and woven into the fabric of reality.

The distinction between male and female does nothing to undermine the value and dignity of either. Both are made in the image of God. Our equality is secured by that fact alone. No distinction—ethnicity, gender, age, sex—threatens the equality of human beings. All are image bearers. All have equal and immeasurable worth in the sight of God.

Transgender people feel that something is wrong. They say they feel like a woman trapped in a man's body or vice versa. However, in light of God's Story of reality, their diagnosis is incorrect. Gender isn't something to suppress or remove. Human wholeness comes not by denying reality but by accepting it.

For the person struggling with gender identity, God's Story offers an accurate diagnosis *and* the singular cure. Rather than affirming any and all desires as good, Scripture offers this insight: "Let no one say when he is tempted, 'I am being tempted by God,' for God cannot be tempted with evil, and he himself tempts no one. But each person is tempted when he is lured and enticed by his own desire" (James 1:13–14). Not every human desire is proper. Many lead us straight into sin, bringing brokenness into our lives: "Then desire when it has conceived gives birth to sin, and sin when it is fully grown brings forth death" (v. 15). Our transgender friends have a good desire for wholeness, but they've taken it in the wrong direction. The result is sin and brokenness.

Here's the brutal truth. Every contemporary corruption of sex and sexuality—whether pornography, the hookup culture, homosexuality, or transgenderism—is open defiance of our creator. We're not just broken; we're rebellious. Romans 1:21–27 graphically captures humanity's revolt and its results:

> For although [people] knew God, they did not honor him as God or give thanks to him, but they became futile in their thinking, and their foolish hearts were darkened....
>
> Therefore God gave them up in the lusts of their hearts to impurity, to the dishonoring of their bodies among themselves, because they exchanged the truth about God for a lie and worshiped and served the creature rather than the Creator, who is blessed forever! Amen.
>
> For this reason God gave them up to dishonorable passions. For their women exchanged natural relations for those that are contrary to nature; and the men

> likewise gave up natural relations with women and were
> consumed with passion for one another, men commit-
> ting shameless acts with men and receiving in themselves
> the due penalty for their error.

But that's not the end of God's Story! The only thing that will put a fractured human being back together is the One who fashioned him or her. God redeems us from our sin through the work of Christ on the cross. His Story shows us how we were made and how He intended us to function properly.

Gender is a gift. God made us male and female, and the unique design and functioning of the sexes isn't something to eradicate. It's a good gift to celebrate.

Action Steps

1. Let God move you to compassion for those who struggle with gender-identity issues. Our transgender friends are hurting. Forty-one percent will attempt suicide compared to just 1.6 percent of the general population. They need friends, as we all do, who will love them well. So, spend time getting to know them. Listen carefully to hear what's going on deep down in their souls. Pray for them often.

2. Speak the truth carefully, with an extra dose of compassion. Culture affirms and celebrates transgender confusion. Few people are willing to tell the truth. Affirm the goodness of what transgender people are seeking: wholeness. However, help them to see that the solution isn't in making changes to their bodies but transforming their hearts, minds, and souls. In every conversation, show grace, kindness, and love.

3. Get a better understanding of gender-identity development. When you grasp how God has designed the family to build healthy gender identity, it will help you understand your friends' and maybe even your own struggles with this issue. Here are two of the most helpful talks on the subject:

- *Why? Understanding Homosexuality and Gender Development in Males*—https://livehope.org/resource/why-dvd/
- *Why? Understanding Homosexuality and Gender Development in Females*—https://livehope.org/resource/femaledvd/

Get online, buy them, watch them with your family or friends, and then discuss.

4. Build loving relationships with your parents. God has designed families to help meet our deepest needs. Students who have a loving relationship with their parents lay a lifelong foundation for physical, psychological, and spiritual health. Do your part. And seek their guidance about gender, relationships, and any questions you have about your sexuality.

Hopecasting

There are brave men and women who have committed themselves to speaking truth on this issue, refusing to be bullied by culture. Walt Heyer, a husband and father of two children, previously identified as a transgender woman but has transitioned back. He now publicly shares his heartbreaking yet hopeful story and regularly addresses contemporary transgender issues.[8]

Dr. Paul McHugh has spent more than forty years as the Distinguished Service Professor of Psychiatry at Johns Hopkins University School of Medicine. For much of that time, he has studied transgenderism and sex-reassignment surgery, working closely with many transgender individuals.

Dr. McHugh is an expert on the subject who speaks out on the damage it can cause, but he's taking plenty of heat. What motivates Dr. McHugh to speak the truth and risk his reputation? "I do so not only because truth matters, but also because overlooked amid the hoopla ... stand many victims.... [Transgenderism] is doing much damage to families, adolescents, and children and should be confronted as an opinion without biological foundation wherever it emerges."[9]

Neither of these men is motivated by hatred. Rather, they're compelled by their compassion for people who are hurting. With the same truth-in-love approach, we can navigate gender identity.

Chapter Eleven

Affluence and Consumerism

"Indeed, if we consider ... the staggering nature of the rewards promised in the Gospels, it would seem that Our Lord finds our desires not too strong, but too weak. We are half-hearted creatures, fooling about with drink and sex and ambition when infinite joy is offered us, like an ignorant child who wants to go on making mud pies in a slum because he cannot imagine what is meant by the offer of a holiday at the sea."

C. S. Lewis, *The Weight of Glory and Other Addresses*

Americans love stuff. We even have "temples" where we go to worship our stuff and then buy more of it. We call them malls!

When you think about it, much of our life is aimed at making money and buying things. How would most of your friends answer the question, "Why do you go to school?" To get into college. Why? To get an education. Why? To get a good job. Why? To make money. Why? To buy what they need, yes, but more importantly, to buy what they *want*.

In fact, the majority of your generation says that success is the highest priority in life. "Two thirds want to finish their education (66%), start a career (66%), and become financially independent (65%) by age 30."[1] Of course, none of those things is bad in and of itself. However, compare this to other life goals. Only 16 percent of teenagers say that becoming spiritually mature is important.[2] Even marriage is low on the list of priorities, with only 20 percent of teens wanting to get married by age 30.[3] Faith and family are taking a huge back seat to financial success.

Our culture tells us that acquiring wealth and possessions is not only the path to true happiness but also an important part of our identity. Buying certain brands and products communicates our value and status to the world. The celebrities we follow on social media often flaunt their possessions as proof of their success and significance. The shoes or makeup you wear, or the phone you use, can give your social status a huge boost. In the process, you're tempted to think you are the sum total of your wealth and possessions. And you attempt to further validate your existence by buying and consuming more. This has become the American Dream.

But do our mountains of stuff really make us happy?

Don't Buy the Cultural Lies

Lie #1: The more you have, the happier you'll be.

Today, we have more money, material goods, technology, leisure time, square footage in our homes, cool vacations, computers, cars, and conveniences than any civilization in human history. As a result, we're happier and more fulfilled than previous generations, right? Wrong.

Americans today report more symptoms of depression and anxiety than over the past fifty years. Antidepressant use has increased almost 400 percent among all ages in the past two decades.[4] Teen depression has increased dramatically over the past five decades and is the most common mental-health disorder among US teens.[5]

Surely middle- and upper-class kids, with their wealth and education, are protected from these struggles. Not at all. In *The Price of Privilege*, Madeline Levine found the opposite to be true:

> America's newly identified at-risk group is preteens and teens from affluent, well-educated families. In spite of their economic and social advantages, they experience among the highest rates of depression, substance abuse, anxiety disorders, somatic complaints, and unhappiness

of any group of children in this country. When researchers look at kids across the socioeconomic spectrum, they
find that the most troubled adolescents often come from
the affluent homes.[6]

Lie #2: You are what you own.

Think about the brands or celebrities you follow on social media. What do
their posts sell? They want you to *identify* with their brand.

Certain brands and products communicate value and status to the
world. People attempt to validate their existence by acquiring material
goods they don't really need or can't afford.

Beneath consumerism, idolatry lurks. It sells an approach to life that
says, "I'm the center of the universe." We seek identity in our stuff because
it validates our worship of self. Reinforced by media, entertainment, and
the endless stream of advertising, we devour goods, services, and even
people in an attempt to satisfy our souls.

However, when we've exhausted the fleeting pleasures of affluence and
consumerism, what remains? Boredom, depression, and meaninglessness.
As a wise man once wrote, "I have seen everything that is done under the
sun, and behold, all is vanity and a striving after wind" (Eccl. 1:14).

But there's a silver lining. When we've exhausted ourselves with the
resources of this world, we look beyond this world. We were called to
create—not consume. God didn't design us to be only takers; He created
us to be makers. As preacher Charles Spurgeon said, "Nothing teaches
us about the preciousness of the Creator as much as when we learn the
emptiness of everything else."[7]

Recapture the Wonder of God's Story

Happiness hasn't always had the contorted meaning it now has in contemporary culture. The "pursuit of happiness" in the Declaration of Independence
wasn't the unchecked pursuit of wealth, pleasure, and personal satisfaction.

Happiness was found in a life well lived, marked by wisdom, virtue, and character. The Old Testament writers had a word for it: *shalom*.

Shalom indicates how life is supposed to be: a life in which human beings flourish. It's a life of wholeness, peace, and delight. In other words, *shalom* is the way things ought to be, according to God's design for life.

A vivid picture of *shalom* is painted in Psalm 1:

> Blessed is the man
> > who walks not in the counsel of the wicked,
> nor stands in the way of sinners,
> > nor sits in the seat of scoffers;
> but his delight is in the law of the LORD,
> > and on his law he meditates day and night.
>
> He is like a tree
> > planted by streams of water
> that yields its fruit in its season. (vv. 1–3)

Shalom represents human flourishing and is found in God's plan of creation, redemption, and restoration.

The New Testament continues to paint this picture. In the Sermon on the Mount, Jesus examined the question of which life is the good life. Over and over, He used the Greek term for "blessed"—*makarios*, which is akin to the Hebrew word *shalom*. According to Jesus, "blessedness," the goal of Christian living, is human flourishing.

In God's Story, human flourishing is grounded in God Himself. As the psalmist said, "For me it is good to be near God" (Ps. 73:28). He is our highest good. Our souls are thirsty for fulfillment. Wealth and possessions are false gods unable to quench that thirst. God is the one who fills us, not earthly goods.

We were designed in God's image and made for relationship with Him. We were also tasked with caring for His creation (Gen. 1:28–30).

Certainly, God created good things for us to consume and enjoy (vv. 29–30), but that isn't the goal of life. We're also to give back.

God's prophets continually warned the people of Israel how life could go wrong. Pleasure itself isn't the problem. God created us with the capacity for pleasure because He is good. For example, good cooks enjoy the food they prepare, and even more, we experience pleasure by seeing others enjoy the things we make.

Wealth isn't necessarily evil, but loving wealth more than God or others is. God has given some of His servants an amazing capacity to create wealth, and as they do, they donate money and hire more workers to lift others out of poverty. There's nothing evil about that at all. We're blessed to be a blessing to others.

But because we're so tempted by possessions and wealth, Jesus gave us plenty of warnings:

- Do not lay up for yourselves treasures on earth, where moth and rust destroy and where thieves break in and steal, but lay up for yourselves treasures in heaven, where neither moth nor rust destroys and where thieves do not break in and steal. For where your treasure is, there your heart will be also. (Matt. 6:19–21)
- No one can serve two masters, for either he will hate the one and love the other, or he will be devoted to the one and despise the other. You cannot serve God and money. Therefore I tell you, do not be anxious about your life, what you will eat or what you will drink, nor about your body, what you will put on. Is not life more than food, and the body more than clothing? (vv. 24–25)

Simply put, affluence and consumption are poor substitutes for God. Jesus put it this way: "If anyone would come after me, let him deny himself and take up his cross daily and follow me. For whoever would save his life will lose it, but whoever loses his life for my sake will save it. For what does it profit a man if he gains the whole world and loses or forfeits himself?" (Luke 9:23–25).

Jesus wasn't giving a command; He was describing reality. We can accumulate all the riches of the world and never achieve the "good life."

Action Steps

1. The first step in our consumer-driven culture is to repent of our own sinful pursuit of affluence. It's easy to absorb our culture's values. We must do the hard work of looking at our own lives, repenting of our love of stuff so we can resist our culture's worship of affluence and pleasure.

2. Learn to say no to your desires. Our culture tells us that if we can buy it, then by definition it's right to do so. Why deny yourself, right? But that's exactly what Jesus tells us to do. Resist the urge to buy something just because you can. Think through your purchases by asking questions like:

- Do I really need this right now? Can it wait?
- Will this purchase help me love God and love my neighbors better?
- Are there better ways I can use the money that I would spend on this?

Building habits of self-control and discipline will help you honor God with your money and material things. And by saying no to yourself (or at least waiting), you'll discover the benefits of delayed gratification.

3. Pay for the things you want. It's not wrong to desire clothing or see the value of the newest tech. But instead of bugging your parents to buy it, plan to save for your purchase. Wise money management includes understanding that responsibility precedes privilege. And you'll experience dignity from working hard and earning things on your own, rather than merely having stuff handed to you.

4. Create a budget. To understand the purpose of money, create a budget using three categories: giving, saving, and spending. Giving is first because all we have comes from God. Really, we are just managing what He has given. Second, it's wise to save for future needs or emergencies. Third, use your remaining finances for personal needs and desires.

5. Avoid debt. Culture tempts us with instant gratification. Borrowing money to buy stuff we want *now* is a huge temptation. But Scripture warns "the borrower is the slave of the lender" (Prov. 22:7). Don't become a slave to your stuff by going into debt to get it.

6. Give things away regularly. Weed out clothes, tech gadgets, and other possessions that you no longer use. Take the items to a local charity or shelter, or give them to a single parent your family knows from church. By releasing your possessions, you prevent those things from controlling you.

7. Expose yourself to the reality of poverty. If you live in a comfortable suburb, it's easy to be insulated from the harsh realities of the world. Get involved in church programs to help the poor. Look to participate in missions or work trips. Volunteer with your friends at a local shelter or food bank.

8. Practice gratitude on a daily basis. Use your prayer time as an opportunity to pause and recognize God's good gifts. Thank Him every day for the specific things He has provided.

Hopecasting

There are hopeful signs that the consumerism of our culture is changing. The millennial generation before you may be more generous than previous generations. In 2014, researchers discovered:

- 84 percent of millennials made a charitable donation.
- 70 percent spent at least an hour volunteering for a cause they cared about.[8]

That's a good start. Your generation can do even more. Be an example to your friends and family by modeling lives of flourishing as you live for the sake of Jesus' kingdom.

Chapter Twelve

Addiction

"My dad was an addict and an alcoholic. Guess I always searched for what he found in drugs and alcohol because ... he chose that over a family."
Demi Lovato, singer, *Simply Complicated*

Our culture increasingly struggles to find true value and purpose but comes up empty.

According to many psychologists, we've become a culture of empty selves. We express and cope with our inner emptiness in myriad ways, and today, more students are turning to drugs and alcohol to soothe their souls.

In a culture of increasing acceptance of drugs and alcohol, how do you keep from being wiped out by this big cultural wave?

Don't Buy the Cultural Lies

Lie #1: Drug and alcohol abuse aren't that big of a problem.
Our culture tends to dismiss drug and alcohol abuse as a fairly small problem. Recent headlines, however, have highlighted a growing epidemic throughout the United States:

- "Americans Are Drinking More—a Lot More"[1]
- "Daily Marijuana Use among College Students at Highest Rate in 35 Years"[2]
- "Heroin: The Poisoning of America"[3]

- "U.S. Opioid Addiction Crisis Is Top Health Story of 2018"[4]

In a survey of high school students, researchers found over a twelve-month stretch:

- 58 percent of twelfth graders used alcohol.
- 35 percent of twelfth graders used marijuana.
- 7 percent of twelfth graders used amphetamines.
- Nearly 24 percent of twelfth graders used illicit drugs.[5]

An increasing number of students abuse all kinds of substances, not just alcohol. The list includes sedatives, tranquilizers, cocaine, club drugs, bath salts, painkillers, opioids, methamphetamines, heroin, hallucinogens, inhalants, and more.

Lie #2: Legal drugs and alcohol are primarily used for recreational purposes.

Look carefully at alcohol advertisements. What do you see? Groups of beautiful people smiling and having the time of their lives. Culture communicates that alcohol, in all its forms, is a harmless means to fun.

Increasingly, marijuana is perceived in the same way. As of 2019, thirty-three states and the District of Columbia allow legal medicinal marijuana. A growing number of states—Alaska, California, Colorado, Oregon, Maine, Massachusetts, Michigan, Nevada, Vermont, and Washington—have legalized recreational marijuana.

When you look underneath the slick alcohol advertisements and the growing chorus of approval for marijuana, you'll discover a massive amount of damage that these substances cause when they're abused. For example, college-age students have reported assaults (including sexual assaults and rape), unintentional injuries, academic problems, unsafe sex, health problems, property damage, confrontations with the police, and deaths, all related to alcohol abuse.[6]

Marijuana isn't harmless either. Today's marijuana products are much more potent, with higher levels of tetrahydrocannabinol (THC). This psychoactive ingredient in marijuana has been shown to be addictive, mind altering, and harmful to the brain, resulting in detrimental cognitive and psychological effects.[7]

In the state of Colorado, the legalization of recreational marijuana in 2013 led to a number of unanticipated problems. Marijuana-related hospitalizations tripled, emergency-room visits increased 30 percent, drug-related school suspensions increased, drug cartels began operations in the state, and drug-related crime increased.[8]

And this doesn't even account for the destruction that illegal substances cause. A heroin epidemic is breaking out in places like Ohio, New Hampshire, and West Virginia. In Huntington, West Virginia, "one in four residents … is hooked on heroin or some other opioid."[9]

As followers of Jesus Christ, we know there's a more foundational matter than physical harm that must be dealt with. In a culture of isolation and fragmentation, people search for something to save them from their pain. For many, drugs and alcohol become substitute saviors. However, using substances as a replacement for the real Savior only dulls life for a few fleeting moments and doesn't satisfy empty souls. Real rescue can be found only in God's Story.

Recapture the Wonder of God's Story

Jesus came for the wounded and broken. When the self-righteous Pharisees questioned Jesus about who He was hanging out with (outcasts, tax collectors, and other sinners), He made His mission clear: "Those who are well have no need of a physician, but those who are sick. I came not to call the righteous, but sinners" (Mark 2:17).

Society is desperately sick. Some seek salvation in sex or consumption, while others turn to substance abuse. However, these false gods cannot give "liberty to the captives" (Luke 4:18). As Peter preached in the book of Acts, "There is salvation in no one else, for there is no other name under heaven given among men by which we must be saved" (4:12).

In God's Story, Jesus rescues, redeems, and reconciles addicts to their creator. And the good news gets even better. The addicted and sinners of all stripes can now say, "I have been crucified with Christ. It is no longer I who live, but Christ who lives in me" (Gal. 2:20).

When you pray to Jesus, admitting your sin and asking for forgiveness (regardless of your past), not only are you saved from your old life of sin and corruption; you're saved to a new life in Christ. You're a new creation (2 Cor. 5:17), and that means there's a new way to be human.

In the old life, sin controlled you (Rom. 6). In this new life, you discover the fruit of self-control as you allow the Holy Spirit to control you (Gal. 5:23). Living a self-controlled life in the power of the Spirit is the emphasis of the New Testament. That's why Paul warns Christians not to "get drunk with wine, for that is debauchery, but be filled with the Spirit" (Eph. 5:18).

Drunkenness is one way we give control of ourselves to something other than God. In contrast, "if the Spirit of him who raised Jesus from the dead dwells in [us], he who raised Christ Jesus from the dead will also give life to [our] mortal bodies through his Spirit who dwells in [us]" (Rom. 8:11). A Spirit-filled, self-controlled new life brings wholeness to body and soul.

Interestingly, the Bible never condemns drinking alcohol. However, it *does* address underage drinking when it tells us to obey the laws of the land and respect the government authorities (Rom. 13:1–3). And God's Word definitely condemns drunkenness (Eph. 5:18; Prov. 20:1).

Moderation is a virtue in the New Testament rather than total self-denial, which applies as much to the glutton as it does to the drunkard. God encourages the proper use of food and drink (see Col. 2:20–23), not the abuse of them. Paul pointed out that the just-say-no approach alone isn't an adequate model of sanctification.

You may find yourself in a time and place when it will be wise to abstain from certain things that aren't sinful in and of themselves. For instance, it's wise for the recovering addict to avoid addictive substances altogether. In addition, it's right for a mature Christian to abstain from food or drink when partaking would cause a brother or sister to stumble (Rom. 14:13–23).

Does the Bible condemn recreational drug use? The very intent of using recreational marijuana,[10] cocaine, heroin, or other illicit substances is to become intoxicated. Therefore, drugs cannot be used in moderation because of their inherently intoxicating nature, which directly opposes the biblical teaching on self-control. Thus, Scripture prohibits drug use.

God is after a renovation of the heart, one filled with the Holy Spirit and able to exert self-control from the inside out. In turn, self-control allows you to live in God's good world while properly enjoying God's good things: Self-control is a mark of maturity in the believer's life and characteristic of godliness (2 Pet. 1:3–7). This is the new kind of Spirit-empowered life that Jesus made possible.

Growing more like God is a lifelong process with many ups and downs. We must honestly assess where we are on that journey, seek the counsel of more mature brothers and sisters in Christ, and act accordingly. Thankfully, God's Story can find us in the midst of the messiness and brokenness of life and move us toward the health and wholeness found only in the gospel of Jesus.

Action Steps

1. If you're struggling with any kind of substance abuse, get help now.
God doesn't want you to run from Him; He wants you to run *to* Him. If you're struggling, go to God in prayer. Confess your sin. And then share your struggles with a parent, mentor, and/or trusted friend. God doesn't

want you to face this alone, and honestly, trying to overcome substance abuse by yourself is nearly impossible. We need others who will lovingly, yet firmly, walk with us.

2. Go beyond "just say no." Rules and boundaries are important, but the power of the Holy Spirit working in our hearts and minds brings lasting change. If you or your friends are dipping your toes into the dangerous waters of drugs or alcohol, turn to God through Bible study, prayer, worship, fasting, and service. Instead of numbing your pain with drugs or alcohol, give your pain to God as you spend time with Him. Also, don't be afraid to ask your parents to give you a hand in finding professional help. Addiction is a real problem. Christian therapists and counselors can be a tremendous help.

3. Be wise about the situations you put yourself in. If you find yourself at a party where people are drinking alcohol or using drugs, get out. And if you know beforehand, don't put yourself in situations where you'll be tempted. Yes, maybe some friends will give you a hard time, but stand firm. Whether they'll admit it or not, people will actually respect you for your convictions and your ability to live them out consistently. They certainly don't respect hypocrisy.

4. Invite your friends over. You can't prevent alcohol from being served at someone else's party, but you can keep it out of yours. And there are plenty of students who don't want to be tempted by substances either. So gather at your place where you can watch a movie, play games, or hang out and talk, without the pressure and presence of alcohol and drugs.

5. Make your family dinners a priority. Teens who had infrequent family dinners (two or fewer per week) were more than twice as likely to use alcohol and marijuana than kids who regularly ate dinner with their families (five to seven times per week).[11] What's the connection? It's not the mere act of eating together that powerfully impacts you. Building strong family relationships over a meal is what protects students from the sway of culture. Make yourself available for meals, and take the lead with your family if necessary.

Hopecasting

I Am Second is a movement that proclaims the power of the gospel. Film actors, athletes, musicians, business leaders, and drug addicts tell their stories of redemption and restoration. Their YouTube testimonials get hundreds of thousands of views online.

One of the most powerful I Am Second stories is the testimony of Brian "Head" Welch, the lead guitarist for the successful nu-metal band Korn. Watch it![12] Brian, tatted up from head to toe, shares his dark journey from famed rock star to full-on addict. He was addicted to cocaine, alcohol, pills, and finally, to the drug that nearly destroyed his life: methamphetamines. In the midst of Welch's personal destruction and despair, Jesus Christ rescued him. It's an amazing account of the power of the gospel. Stories like Welch's confirm the power of God's Story to transform anyone's story, no matter how broken.

Chapter Thirteen

Entertainment

"Movies can and do have tremendous influence in shaping young lives in the realm of entertainment towards the ideals and objectives of normal adulthood."
Walt Disney

The Star Wars movies have grossed over $9 billion worldwide. They're one of the largest movie franchises in history. Movie producer George Lucas, who created Star Wars, recognized these movies as more than mere entertainment: "[Star Wars is] designed primarily to make young people think about the mystery. Not to say, 'Here's the answer.' It's to say, 'Think about this for a second. Is there a God? What does God look like? What does God sound like? What does God feel like? How do we relate to God?'"[1]

All entertainment, whether it's music, movies, TV shows, video games, or YouTube videos, is loaded with ideas with the power to shape us. Just take any popular song over the last few years and read the lyrics without the music playing. Do lyrics communicate ideas? Listen to Bruno Mars and Cardi B in their 2019 hit song "Please Me":

> You know what I want and what I need, baby …
> I'm gonna ride it, do it just how you like it
> Tonight and after that
> Let's do it one more time
> Girl, I ain't one for beggin', but now you got me
>   beggin'.[2]

If you've heard the full song, you know we've left out the most explicit lyrics. And that's one example of literally thousands of songs produced each year, promoting all kinds of messages about human sexuality. The "Please Me" music video has more than 240 million views on YouTube. When you can get that many people listening to your song, that's huge influence. So, are musicians interested in more than just entertaining? Absolutely.

Entertainment has become an overwhelming cultural force. There's nothing in Western civilization that rivals the power of entertainment to shape what we think and how we think.

Don't Buy the Cultural Lies

Lie #1: Relax! It's just entertainment.

Certainly, entertainment is enjoyable. But that's not the complete story, and entertainers themselves realize it. Musician and actress Courtney Love, wife of the late Kurt Cobain of Nirvana, rose to prominence in the 1990s and has continued to act and produce music. In an interview with *Spin* magazine, Courtney was clear: "I feel like I have a duty. I as an architect have a need to impose my worldview on the culture."[3]

Often, the message of a movie or song isn't straightforward. The ideas and worldviews are disguised within the entertainment. For instance, we're taught as children that bad guys are bad. There's a clear line between good and evil. But the movie *Ocean's Eleven* paints the professional criminals played by George Clooney and Brad Pitt as heroes. By the end of the movie, we're cheering for them to steal millions of dollars. Or take the hit TV show *Modern Family*. Alongside a traditional family, there are a divorce/remarriage/trophy-wife family and a gay couple. Take your pick. Any of these portrayals of "modern family" life are just as legitimate as any other.

Over time, these ideas trickle into the conscience of the culture. Slowly but surely, they shape our views of the world, standards of acceptable behavior, and our identities. "We become what we behold."[4] We created entertainment, and now entertainment is re-creating us.

Lie #2: The medium is neutral.

No R-rated movies. No explicit lyrics. As long as we avoid sex, drugs, and violence, entertainment is harmless, for the most part, right? So as long as we avoid the really bad stuff, we can watch, listen, tweet, and post away! This approach sounds good, but it underestimates the nature of technology.

What's the primary medium (or means) through which entertainment is delivered? The screen. It accomplishes its task through images (pictures and video).

Images make your mind passive—not active. Watching flickering images on a screen doesn't require much mental effort: we simply absorb what is presented. Thus, screens change us from participants into spectators. The screen comes on, and our minds turn off. Images come fast and furious, so we tend not to think carefully about what we're viewing. Screens literally make us dumber.[5]

Entertainment can also lead to addiction. We watch our screens to cure boredom or avoid responsibility. Through streaming video and music services, we try to escape reality and can easily lose track of time. We start watching one episode and that quickly turns into six.

Recapture the Wonder of God's Story

Jesus said, "Man shall not live by bread alone, but by every word that comes from the mouth of God" (Matt. 4:4). If our most important nourishment is found not in physical food but in God and His Word, what does that imply about the entertainment culture?

First, we must return to the basis of our identity. We are made in the image of God (Gen. 1:26). Like God Himself, image bearers were made to create, not just consume. We were designed to work. From our efforts in school, our jobs, and through extracurricular activities, we can create good things. We're to have "dominion" over the earth (v. 28). But when we constantly consume entertainment, we allow the things of this world to have dominion over us.

This isn't to say all entertainment is bad. Indeed, creating art is the activity of image bearers, and art can be entertaining. The world needs good art to stir and shape the imagination. A good song can move our emotions. A well-produced film can evoke feelings of joy or preserve important cultural memories.

Producing a film, writing a song, or painting a picture doesn't have to be separate from our life in Christ. Creative pursuits should be done with and for Christ. As the apostle Paul reminds us: "Whatever you do, in word or deed, do everything in the name of the Lord Jesus, giving thanks to God the Father through him" (Col. 3:17). Our good creations point us back to a good God and bring Him glory. "So, whether you eat or drink, or whatever you do, do all to the glory of God" (1 Cor. 10:31).

Our minds play a central role in our spiritual growth. Paul told us that we're "transformed by the renewal of [our minds]" (Rom. 12:2). The question isn't *if* our minds are being renewed; it's by what. As we consume entertainment, our minds are being renewed. Yet as we've seen, much of what our entertainment culture produces actually harms our spiritual growth. Instead, God calls us to think about "whatever is true, whatever is honorable, whatever is just, whatever is pure, whatever is lovely, whatever is commendable ... [whatever is excellent and] worthy of praise" (Phil. 4:8). Entertainment that tells God's True Story can renew our minds with His truth, goodness, and beauty.

Action Steps

1. Take regular breaks from entertainment. Create sacred spaces that are screen-free. Make the kitchen table, living room, or your bedroom a space where you don't let screens in. Instead, make them places to talk, read, write, think, or pray. Or get a little radical and set aside an entire day once a week to take a total break from entertainment. Pausing entertainment will help prevent addiction to it. And it may reveal how prevalent it has become in your life.

2. Become aware of your entertainment diet. Make a list of your favorite songs, TV shows, movies, and YouTube channels. Evaluate the content. Is that reality show or Netflix series good for your heart and mind? You may even want to pull in a parent or youth leader for an outside opinion. Identify the junk and cut it out of your entertainment diet.

3. Actively engage entertainment rather than passively absorb it. Don't allow culture to think for you. When you watch a movie or TV show, hit the pause button once in a while and think about what you just saw. Engage your mind, instead of turning it off. Use this list of questions to evaluate your entertainment:

- What is the main story line and/or overarching theme?
- How are the characters portrayed? Who are the good guys? Who are the bad guys?
- What values are promoted directly or indirectly?
- What is the good life according to the movie?
- What messages about human sexuality are being promoted?
- Are there any religious references? If so, what is said and how is religion portrayed?
- How do the messages match up with Scripture?

Before you add a song to your playlist, look up the lyrics and read them carefully. If they don't communicate truth and goodness, make the mature decision and ditch the song.

4. Redeem screen time. There are certainly entertainment choices we need to say no to, but we also need to seek out music, movies, and TV shows we can say yes to. Look for entertainment that is thoughtful, communicates truth, and encourages goodness. Don't settle for distraction, triviality, or messages that push sin.

5. Look for alternatives to entertainment. Move beyond the screen. Engage your own creativity instead of consuming all the time. Take music lessons. Make films. Buy an art easel and paint. Learn a new sport. Enjoy a board game with friends. Read a book. When you turn off the screen, it's okay if you feel bored at first. Often boredom is the first step to opening up your imagination and unlocking your creativity.

6. Get outside. Most of us suffer from NDD—*nature deficit disorder*. Go to the park, the mountains, or the beach. Go on a walk, hike, or bike ride. Bring some friends with you.

7. Develop a reading habit. Books don't merely entertain; some teach truth. And they do so not through images but by language. The words in a book force your mind to work harder. As you read, your mind is active, not passive, as it translates the words into concepts and ideas. For this reason, if you haven't developed a habit of reading, it may be challenging to get started. Just as an out-of-shape person struggles the first few times back at the gym, an underactive mind needs time to get in shape. But the hard work is worth it! Reading grows your mind in ways images can't.

Hopecasting

Remember, followers of Jesus are to be in the world but not of it. The culture desperately needs more Christians redeeming entertainment by creating beautiful art to the glory of God. That doesn't mean slapping Bible verses on a film or merely inserting "Jesus" into song lyrics. Thankfully, there are artists you can follow as models of cultural engagement.

Lecrae is a multi-award-winning hip-hop artist, the cofounder of Reach Records, and a devoted follower of Jesus Christ. His 2014 album, *Anomaly*, debuted at number one on the Billboard 200. His lyrics depart from the money-sex-violence formula that typifies many hip-hop songs. Instead, he expresses gratitude for the Redeemer, discusses social issues like adultery and abortion, and warns about sin. Twenty One Pilots is a top-notch, commercially successful rock band. Singer Tyler Joseph and drummer Josh Dun are committed Christians who have avoided the "Christian band" label and the mainstream marginalization that comes with it. However, their songs are filled with truth as they open up about fear, doubt, anxiety, and insecurity.

Lecrae, Tyler Joseph, and Josh Dun are artists doing excellent work as Christians. Driven by the truth of the Christian worldview, these artists are engaging and redeeming our entertainment culture with exceptional art. At the same time, they're telling God's Story from a huge mainstream platform. Lecrae explains:

> We've limited Christianity to salvation and sanctification.… Christianity is the truth about everything. If you say you have a Christian worldview, that means you see the world through that lens—not just how people get saved and what to stay away from.… Christians need to embrace that there need to be believers talking about love and social issues and all other aspects of life.[6]

Chapter Fourteen

Racial Tension

*"There are no ordinary people. You have never
talked to a mere mortal. Nations, cultures,
arts, civilisations—these are mortal, and
their life is to ours as the life of a gnat. But
it is immortals whom we joke with, work
with, marry, snub, and exploit—immortal
horrors or everlasting splendours."*

C. S. Lewis, *The Weight of Glory
and Other Addresses*

Many Americans hoped the election of Barack Obama, the first African American president, in 2008 would finally bring racial reconciliation to our country. However, high-profile police shootings of African Americans, followed by protests and riots, revealed that our country is still very much divided on the issue of race.

Racial divisions aren't unique to the United States. The modern world is filled with strife between groups, from the streets of Palestine to the tensions between North and South Korea to the conflict between the Kurds and the Turks. In the recent past, racial conflict in Rwanda, Bosnia, and Darfur (Sudan) resulted in unspeakable violence and genocide. Chechnya. France. India. Sri Lanka. Russia. Bolivia. Belgium. Great Britain. Racial strife isn't an American problem; it's a human problem.

Don't Buy the Cultural Lies

Lie #1: You are your ethnicity.

Culture says our identity is linked to our racial group—Chinese, Mexican, Egyptian, Russian, Swedish, African, and so on. Racial identity is in our genes, and therefore, our primary identity is based on our ethnicity.

However, the biological differences between ethnic groups are minuscule. Researchers involved with the Human Genome Project say, "If you ask what percentage of your genes is reflected in your external appearance, the basis by which we talk about race, the answer seems to be in the range of .01 percent."[1] Researchers concluded, "There is only one race—the human race." Overly identifying with an ethnic identity makes racial divisions worse.

Lie #2: Racism is not that big of a problem, so people need to get over it.

In the view of some, we've largely solved the race problem in our country, so now it's time for people to get over it and quit playing the race card. However, if racism is discrimination against someone of a different ethnicity based on a belief in one's own racial superiority, how can anyone deny that racism still exists? There are plenty of examples:

- Police officials in the city of Ferguson, Missouri, circulating racially charged emails.[2]
- University of Oklahoma fraternity students chanting, "There will never be a ni**** SAE [Sigma Alpha Epsilon]. You can hang him from a tree, but he can never sign with me."[3]
- Two white protestors at an "impeach Trump" rally telling a black Fox News contributor to "Go back to Kenya."[4]

Better yet, ask friends of a different ethnicity if they've experienced racism and they'll likely have a few stories to share. Personal stories hit home and help us see that racism is alive and well.

Racial divisions are hardly behind us, so it does no good to pretend they are. Racism is detestable. Racism is sin. And racism is a reality.

Lie #3: Racism in the United States is happening everywhere all the time. From conflicts with police to campus protests to violent riots, the media paints a picture that the entire country is engulfed in racial strife. Of course, no one can deny incidents of racial tension.

While racial tensions continue to flare up, America has made significant progress over the past fifty years. In 1991, Harvard sociologist Orlando Patterson, an African American, declared, "America, while still flawed in its race relations … is now the least racist white-majority society in the world."[5]

The *New York Times* reported that the freshman class to Congress in 2018 was the most racially diverse, with twenty-four people of color being elected.[6]

Certainly, there is an ongoing need for constructive conversations on race relations. But it's noteworthy that immigrants from other nations still flock to the United States—and prosper here.

Recapture the Wonder of God's Story

Christians must be vigilant not to absorb racialized views of the culture. To accomplish this, our perspectives on race relations must start and end with God's Word.

Addressing the unbelievers in Athens, Greece, the apostle Paul highlighted God's Story of humanity's origin: "[God] made from one man every nation of mankind to live on all the face of the earth, having determined allotted periods and the boundaries of their dwelling place.… 'For we are indeed his offspring'" (Acts 17:26, 28). In God's Story, there is one human race.

C. S. Lewis communicated this biblical truth in The Chronicles of Narnia, addressing the Pevensie children as the "sons of Adam" and "daughters of Eve." These dignified titles acknowledge our shared humanity as descendants of the original image bearers.

God's Story begins not with the racial superiority of some and the inferiority of others, but with the value and equality of all humanity. People of color—all colors!—are precious in His sight.

It's important to note that we not only share Adam's humanness; we also inherit his fallenness: "Sin came into the world through one man, and death through sin, and so death spread to all men because all sinned" (Rom. 5:12). As a result of sin, humanity began to fracture. The Old Testament is filled with stories of hostility in human relationships, depicted through ethnic divisions, animosity, and bloodshed.

So where can followers of Christ find a road map to change thousands of years of racial strife? The answer: the world has never seen a more powerful tool for overcoming ethnic barriers as the gospel of Jesus Christ. In Acts, we see the beautiful transformation of Jewish ethnic segregation into Jesus-centered ethnic acceptance. And it happened within a single generation! Through Christ, "Jews, Gentiles and Samaritans could become a part of God's people without losing their cultural identity."[7]

Interestingly, Luke, more than any other gospel writer, took special notice of the oft-despised Samaritans. Jews saw their Samaritan neighbors as third-class citizens, lower in status than even the Gentiles. But in the book of Luke, Jesus set the stage for the radical movement of the gospel (Luke 9:51–56; 10:26–37; 17:11–19). In the beginning of Acts, Jesus says, "You will be my witnesses in Jerusalem and in all Judea and Samaria, and to the end of the earth" (Acts 1:8).

As God's Story unfolds in Acts, the incredible power of the gospel transcends deep ethnic barriers. Eventually the gospel breaks down Jewish, Samaritan, Roman, Greek, and Ethiopian barriers—and beyond. In Ephesians 2, Paul described how "the dividing wall of [ethnic] hostility" was broken down "by the blood of Christ," resulting in peace as we become "fellow citizens with the saints and members of the household of God" (vv. 13–14, 19).

Notice something very important. The early church didn't have a formal plan to build multiethnic churches. The only plan was to proclaim the gospel. As people pledged their allegiance to Jesus, their loyalty to Christ and His mission took priority over ethnic and cultural loyalties. In Christ, we have the one tool that can ultimately overcome racial strife and tear down ethnic barriers. Imagine what a witness the church would be to a racially divided world if we recaptured that first-century, gospel-centered unity once again.

Action Steps

1. Examine your own views. You need to be brutally honest with yourself. How does skin color or ethnicity shape your assumptions about others? Do you find your identity primarily in your ethnicity or in Jesus Christ? Are your thoughts and feelings marked by forgiveness and reconciliation or hostility and bitterness? Do you simply dismiss all concerns about racism without listening carefully to others?

Followers of Jesus don't have the option of tolerating racial or ethnic barriers. It's sin. We take our cues from Scripture, not culture.

2. Develop genuine friendships with those of other ethnicities. Hang out with your Caucasian, black, Hispanic, or Asian friends. Get coffee or share a meal together. Ask about their experience with racism and listen carefully. Acknowledge there are different racial experiences. You may not agree with other people's perspectives, but their inherent dignity as God's image bearers demands we listen to others and try to understand their perspectives. We can be thankful for our unique ethnic identities while recognizing that our identity in Christ is the most important thing about us.

3. Treat individuals as individuals. Fight racial stereotypes. All ethnicities are tempted to dismiss entire groups of people based on generalizations or personal experiences. Don't judge people on the basis of their race. Instead, give individuals the benefit of the doubt, and get to know them personally.

4. Don't let culture control the conversation on race. Reject cultural values like self-segregation, hostility, resentment, bitterness, victimhood, and entitlement. Instead, let the Bible guide you. It has the resources the world needs for racial reconciliation: insights on the human condition, confession, forgiveness, redemption, unity, the power of the Holy Spirit, and more.

5. Avoid slogans and clichés. Here are some examples:

- We should be color-blind.
- Black lives matter.
- All lives matter.

These phrases are unhelpful not only because they are politicized and can be misunderstood but because they're often used to shut down debate and conversation. The goal for Christians isn't to be blind to color but to embrace the distinctive qualities and uniqueness of God's image bearers.

6. Be on the lookout for other expressions of discrimination besides race. Race is the most obvious area of discrimination in our culture, but there are others. America has problems with classism (looking down on others of lower socioeconomic status), political division (especially after the 2016 election), and sexism (discrimination of men or women). We must address all discrimination and instead look to God's instruction for how to relate to each other in all areas: "Love your neighbor as yourself" (Mark 12:31).

Hopecasting

However, is the portrayal of America as an overtly racist nation accurate?

The facts tell us it isn't. For example, in 1958, only 37 percent of Americans expressed willingness to vote for a black person for president. By 1999, that percentage had risen to 95 percent.[8] Is there hope for a racially divided world? Absolutely. In Revelation, we're given the beautiful vision of the multiethnic new heavens and new earth:

> [The living creatures and twenty-four elders] sang a new song, saying,
>
> "Worthy are you to take the scroll
>   and to open its seals,
> for you were slain, and by your blood you ransomed
>   people for God
>   from every tribe and language and people and
>   nation,
> and you have made them a kingdom and priests to our
>   God,
>   and they shall reign on the earth." (Rev. 5:9–10)

Even now the bride of Christ, the church, can advance the Bible's vision of reconciliation. All "other-isms," including racism, can be defeated with the power of the gospel. Thus, the church should lead in exposing, confronting, and condemning any and all acts of discrimination and dehumanization. We must show a racially divided world a better way.

Part Four

Building a Christian Worldview

Chapter Fifteen

How to Read the Bible

"The secret of my success? It is simple. It is found in the Bible: 'In all thy ways acknowledge Him and He shall direct thy paths.'"

George Washington Carver, acceptance speech for Roosevelt Medal

The Bible, like the uniqueness of Christ, sets Christianity apart from all other worldviews and religions. The Scriptures are essential to knowing God. No new discovery or cultural trend will ever take its place as the primary source of knowledge about reality. Most important, we aren't the authority for determining the best way to live our lives. The Scriptures are.

However, the Bible can be intimidating and confusing. It's hard to know even where to start. So, many find it just easier *not* to read it.

Sadly, even most Christians aren't reading the Bible. Only 14 percent of adults read the Bible daily, 13 percent several times a week, and 8 percent once a week. That means the vast majority of Christian adults aren't reading the Bible regularly.[1]

How about you? Reading the Bible isn't optional for followers of Jesus.

Unless we're immersed in the Scriptures, we'll never have a Christian worldview. In fact, only 4 percent of Gen Z have a biblical worldview.[2] Don't be part of the 96 percent. Read your Bible and let it shape your heart and mind. But as you do, remember these things:

Pray. God has given us the Holy Spirit to guide us and reveal His truth to us. Therefore, as you read God's Word, you're never doing so alone. The Holy Spirit is right there with you. Before you dive in, start by praying and asking the Spirit to open your eyes to God's knowledge and wisdom. Here's a sample prayer you can use:

> God, open my eyes as I read Your Word.
> Give me a passion and love for Your Word.
> I want to know You more and be transformed by Your
> truth.
> Help me to understand Your Word as I keep digging
> into it.
> Help me to obey Your Word as I discover what it
> means.
> Change my heart and mind through Your Word.
> Amen.

The Purpose. The Bible is the true Story of the world. It frames all of reality and shows us the way to join His work. Yet many Christians skip over much of the Old Testament because we don't want to do the hard work of understanding the historical context, and we fail to see its application to the twenty-first century. Instead, we read the "easier" parts of Scripture.

But God gave us *all* of Scripture. As Paul told Timothy, "All Scripture is breathed out by God and profitable for teaching, for reproof, for correction, and for training in righteousness, that the man of God may be complete, equipped for every good work" (2 Tim. 3:16–17). If we aren't learning from all of Scripture, we won't be fully equipped.

The Story. Wherever we are in the biblical text, we should locate where it is in the overall Story. From the creation of the heavens and the earth to the new creation of the new heavens and the new earth, the Bible is the comprehensive and overarching Story of reality from God. The four big chapters—creation, fall, redemption, and restoration—help us to make sense of all the different parts of the story. Every individual sentence and paragraph in the Bible fits into the larger Story, and Jesus is central to that Story.

In Colossians, the apostle Paul offered an incredible description of Jesus' role:

> [Jesus] is the image of the invisible God, the firstborn of all creation. For by him all things were created, in heaven and on earth, visible and invisible, whether thrones or dominions or rulers or authorities—all things were created through him and for him. And he is before all things, and in him all things hold together. And he is the head of the body, the church. He is the beginning, the firstborn from the dead, that in everything he might be preeminent. For in him all the fullness of God was pleased to dwell, and through him to reconcile to himself all things, whether on earth or in heaven, making peace by the blood of his cross. (1:15–20)

The Flow. The Bible is not a collection of verses. It's a collection of books and letters. The chapter and verse divisions were added more than a thousand years after the original writings to help readers find particular sections. However, these verse divisions were never intended to break up the Bible into smaller, more readable parts. If we approach the Bible as a mere collection of verses, we miss the immediate context and overall story and may misunderstand the meaning.

Some books, such as the Psalms and Proverbs, maintain their meaning in bite-size, smaller pieces. But consider a verse like Jeremiah 29:11, "For I know the plans I have for you, declares the LORD, plans for welfare and not for evil, to give you a future and a hope." Some people read that verse and think, *Wow, God has a plan to make everything perfect for me.*

That verse, like every verse in the Bible, has a context. Those words were written when God's people were in exile. God had allowed their nation to be destroyed because of the people's disobedience. They had strayed from God and worshipped idols. Now they were living in a foreign land. Instead of giving up hope, God wanted His people to know that He still had a plan. There was a bright future, but they wouldn't see it overnight. They'd have to wait seventy years (Jer. 29:10).

As Jeremiah 29:11 shows, sometimes the context is in the preceding or following verse. Other times, it's found in another book of the Bible entirely (for example, the gospel writers often referred to Old Testament prophecies or narratives). Generally speaking, if you want to know the meaning of a single verse, you can't just read that verse. You have to know the flow of the surrounding verses.

The Genre. While each of the individual stories of the Bible teaches a good lesson, they shouldn't stand alone. Every story in the Bible is part of a larger story, which is ultimately part of the Story of redemption.

The Bible is an incredibly diverse book of many genres: history, poetry, prophecy, letters, and all types of literature. By reading each part of God's Word as it was intended, you'll gain a better understanding and appreciation.

If you're reading a letter (such as Philippians, Philemon, or 1 Thessalonians), read it like a letter. Ask, "Who wrote this and why? To whom was the author writing?" If it's a poem, read it as poetry. If it's a historical book, read it as history. Ask, "Who is this account about? When did it happen? What was the historical situation behind the book? How does it fit in the overall history of God's redemptive purposes?" Knowing the genre, the type of literature, of a biblical book will help you understand the what, when, where, and why of the text you're reading.

Since God inspired this book, He not only intended what was written; He also intended how it was written.

The Word. Remember to read God's Word *before* turning to any supplemental study notes or commentaries. It's true that God has raised up teachers and preachers to help us, and we should listen to what those leaders have to say, but let the biblical text speak first.

The Christian Community. The Bible is given to His people, not just to individuals. Both the Old and New Testament books were given to communities and were intended to be read aloud. Personal reading is vital, but try to read the Bible with family and friends as much as you can. Discuss it together. Wrestle with it together. Pray through it together.

Tools to Help You Get into God's Word

God's Word is absolutely essential to understanding His Story. Understanding His Story is essential to how we think about and live in His reality. Therefore, we must regularly renew our minds with His truth. It's key to our transformation: "Do not be conformed to this world, but be transformed by the renewal of your mind" (Rom. 12:2). There is no substitute for reading the Bible, so get started.

You can find many Bible reading plans online. Your parents or youth leader may even have some ideas. Plus, there are many helpful Bible resources available. Here are some particularly helpful ones:

- TheBibleProject.com features well-done and easy-to-understand animated videos that explain the background of each biblical book, significant themes in the Bible, and the meaning of important words.
- *The Apologetics Study Bible for Students* edited by Sean McDowell (Holman, 2017) includes introductions and study notes for each book of the Bible, as well as dozens of articles with intelligent and practical answers to students' biggest questions about the Christian faith.
- *The Story: The Bible as One Continuing Story of God and His People* (Zondervan, 2011) condenses the story of the Bible into thirty-one accessible chapters. By arranging the events, characters, and teachings of the Bible in chronological order, it allows the story of Scripture to be read like a novel.

Chapter Sixteen

Why to Trust the Bible

"*Always it is stressed that the claim of the word of God
upon us is absolute: the word is to be received, trusted and
obeyed, because it is the word of God the King.*"

J. I. Packer, *Knowing God*

Christian: God exists and Jesus is the Son of God.

Skeptic: How do you know?

Christian: Because it's in the Bible.

Skeptic: Why should I believe the Bible?

Christian: Because it's the Word of God.

Skeptic: How do you know?

Christian: Because the Bible *says* that it's the Word of God.

Skeptic: What if it's wrong?

Christian: It's not.

Skeptic: How do you know?

Christian: Because the Bible says so.

Have you heard a Christian use that line of reasoning to defend the Bible?
Have *you* used it? If you try to reason like this with your skeptical friends,
they'll likely remain unconvinced. Why? Because it's a circular argument,
which means it relies on itself to prove itself. It assumes the Bible is the
Word of God, when that's what actually needs to be proven. In a culture
where countless voices online, in media, and in school question the Bible's
authority and relevance, followers of Jesus will have to do better.

Key to understanding the authority of Scripture is knowing what the Bible is ... and isn't. The Bible isn't merely a list of rules or a compilation of doctrines, even though it contains both. We've described the Bible as a story (the Story), but we have to be careful what we communicate when we use story language. A story that begins "Once upon a time" doesn't exactly demand respect and obedience. "In the beginning" might, but we need to say more.

Ultimately, the authority of the Bible comes from the God who has given us His Word. That's why words like *inspiration, infallibility*, and *inerrancy* have long been important for Christians. Those words help us get at the nature of the book itself. If the Bible is just another man-made religious text like the Qur'an or the Book of Mormon, then it doesn't hold any authority over us. However, if God spoke His Word through human authors, using their own individual personalities, to write and compose His unique revelation to humankind through the sixty-six books of the Bible, it does hold authority.

So, here are the questions we must answer: Why should we think the Bible is the authoritative source of truth for all humanity? What evidence demonstrates that it's the inspired Word of God?

A Good Argument for the Authority of the Bible

Take the claim that the Bible is divine revelation from God. Certainly, all worldviews cannot make such a claim. For example, the Bible isn't a possibility in an atheistic world. If there's no God, there's no God's Word. A theistic worldview is necessary. Therefore, the first step is to look to natural theology (also called *general revelation*) to see if there are good reasons for believing God exists. Natural theology simply looks at the natural world to discover knowledge about God.

Over the past thirty years, significant contributions from Christian philosophers and scientists have strengthened the arguments for God's existence.[1] The following three arguments not only offer powerful evidence that God exists but also provide clues to His identity and character.

The cosmological argument points to the beginning of the universe as evidence for a Great Beginner. Even the dominant view of origins in current science claims the universe had a beginning. Whoever began the universe must be all-powerful, because He was able to create the universe *ex nihilo* (out of nothing). He must possess great intelligence in order to arrange all the parts of the universe. Lastly, the Beginner must be timeless and immaterial if He existed prior to the creation of time and matter. Already, the Beginner sounds like God.

The fine-tuning argument adds to our information about this Beginner. The universe is incredibly fine-tuned, meaning conditions had to be "just right" to produce life. For example, the gravitational force and expansion rate of the universe had to be constant, and a life-sustaining solar system could have only one star. Scientists tell us there are a multitude of "just right" cosmological constants in the universe that make life on planet Earth possible. The odds of all of these constants happening by chance are basically impossible. Therefore, not only does a finely tuned universe point to the existence of a Fine Tuner, but it also suggests that the Fine Tuner cares about the inhabitants of the universe.

The moral argument points to the character and social nature of the One who began and finely tuned the universe as the best explanation for the existence of moral values. Love and kindness are virtues because they're grounded in God's loving and kind character. The mindless processes of evolution cannot give us moral values or obligations, but an authoritative and morally perfect person can. Therefore, moral laws and obligations are best explained by the existence of a moral Law Giver, who created and rules over the world.

These three arguments not only give us powerful evidence that God exists, but they also tell us He is a transcendent, intelligent, powerful, personal, and moral being. The universe points us to Him. As the apostle Paul said in Romans 1:20: "[God's] invisible attributes, namely, his eternal power and divine nature, have been clearly perceived, ever since the creation of the world, in the things that have been made."

It's also reasonable to think that this personal God would provide additional information about who He is and what His purposes are. We would expect Him to shed some light on humanity's big questions. A caring creator who looks down on a world broken by sin and evil, and knows our trouble, would reveal Himself to us and come to our rescue. And He does—through His Word, the Bible, and His Son, Jesus Christ.

Not only did God give us His Word, but He also passed it down to us in a way we can trust. The trustworthiness of the Bible can be proven in many ways. Here are three:

1. Transmission: Is what we have today what was originally written?
2. Historicity: Is what was written what really happened?
3. Inspiration: Is what was written really from God Himself?

First, when you examine how the Bible has been passed through the ages, you discover that no other ancient document comes close to the accuracy of the biblical text. Thousands upon thousands of manuscript copies and fragments of the Old and New Testaments verify this.[2] Therefore, you can know that what Matthew, Mark, Luke, John, Paul, Peter, and the rest of the biblical authors originally wrote is what you're reading today.

Second, when you look at historical details, you see what was written in the pages of the Bible is accurate and reliable. For example, the Dead Sea Scrolls or the Caiaphas ossuary are just a couple archaeological discoveries that support the historicity of the Bible.[3] There are thousands of others! Therefore, you can trust the Bible is a reliable historical source containing facts about the history of Israel and the life, death, and resurrection of Jesus of Nazareth.

Third, when you look at the nature of the Bible, you find divine fingerprints all over it. For instance, how can a collection of books written by approximately forty different authors on three different continents over a period of more than fifteen hundred years record one unified, coherent story and message? Answer: a divine author was working through human hearts and hands. What explains dozens and dozens of fulfilled biblical prophecies about the person and work of Jesus Christ? Answer: a divine mind who knows the future. This kind of evidence, plus the transforming power of the book in countless lives over two thousand years, provides compelling evidence that the Bible is no ordinary book but the inspired Word of God.

Trust God's Word and Dive In

No other book has been written, passed down, and protected like God's Word. Because God is the highest authority, the Bible is authoritative. Because He is true, good, and beautiful, so is the Bible. The Bible was the first book to come off a printing press and is the bestselling book of all time. The Bible is our ultimate source of knowledge on which we can base our most important beliefs about the world and from which we should test all other knowledge claims.

Don't fear researching the reliability and trustworthiness of the Bible. The arguments in this chapter just scratch the surface of all the evidence that's been uncovered about the trustworthiness of God's Word. Thousands upon thousands of websites and books have been written to defend the Bible and demonstrate its reliability. Here are a few:

- *Cold-Case Christianity: A Homicide Detective Investigates the Claims of the Gospels* by J. Warner Wallace (David C Cook, 2013)
- *Questioning the Bible: 11 Major Challenges to the Bible's Authority* by Jonathan Morrow (Moody, 2014)
- Stand to Reason—www.str.org

Dive into the Bible. Trust it and build your life upon it. There's no other book like it in the world.

Chapter Seventeen

The Right Kind
of Pluralism

*"We believe that all religions are basically the same…. They only differ
on matters of creation, sin, heaven, hell, God, and salvation."*
Steve Turner, "Creed"

Shane was thrilled. He and his girlfriend, Francesca, had just finished
hours of conversation with their skeptical friends at a local restaurant. They
kicked off the conversation by presenting arguments for God's existence.
Eventually, after wrestling with the evidence, their friends acknowledged
that God must exist.

Next, they moved into a conversation about Christianity. After their
friends raised objections to Christian exclusivism with the all-religions-
are-basically-the-same argument, Shane and Francesca discussed the clear
differences among various religious views. Like the quote at the beginning
of this chapter, they pointed out the varying claims of different religions
about God, salvation, and the afterlife. Then they offered some of the evidence for the credibility of Christianity.

Eventually the conversation came to an end, but only after they had
covered a tremendous amount of ground about God and religion.

So who are Shane and Francesca? High school students. You might feel
like a lot of other Christian students who have a difficult time talking with
skeptical friends about Christianity. In our pluralistic society where people
believe many different things about religion, it's difficult to confidently

assert your own beliefs without being labeled close minded or a religious bigot. To share that Jesus is the only way to eternal life, we're told, is the height of intolerance.

Is Christianity exclusively true as Shane and Francesca proclaimed to their skeptical friends, or is it just one religious option among many? Today's young Christians can and should be aware of our religiously diverse culture and yet ready to make a case for the Christian worldview, while recognizing the inherent dignity of all people.

What the Culture Teaches about Religion and Truth

1. All religions are equally true and legitimate paths to God.

Our culture's pluralistic vision states that all religions—Christianity, Judaism, Islam, Hinduism, and Buddhism—lead to the same place. They just take different paths to get there.

Simple logic refutes this view. One of the fundamental laws of logic, the law of noncontradiction, says opposite ideas cannot both be true at the same time and in the same way. And the claims of different religions *are* contradictory. For example, Islam teaches that God is a unitarian being. Christianity teaches that God is Trinitarian (Father, Son, and Holy Spirit). Hinduism and Buddhism say humans are reincarnated after death. Islam and Christianity teach that heaven or hell is our final destination. To say these views are all true at the same time is like claiming two plus two equals four and five. The various religions offer *mutually exclusive* views about God, salvation, the afterlife, and a host of other issues that cannot all be true at the same time.

2. Religion is a matter of personal preference, not objective truth.

You might like chocolate ice cream, while someone else likes vanilla, but neither would claim we have the one true flavor. Many people think about religious claims the way they think about ice cream. Christians have their truth, Muslims have their truth, and so on.

However, this claim is confused about the nature of religious claims, which are grounded not in our individual preferences but in the nature of reality. Religions make objective claims about the nature of God, humanity, salvation, the afterlife, and more. When Christians or Muslims say, "God exists," they make an objective claim about the existence of God, and its truth value is independent from what any of us think or say. Objective claims are either true or false whether anyone believes them or not. Each religion has its take on the true Story of the world. Each is either objectively right or objectively wrong.

3. If you think your religion is the one true religion, you are intolerant.
If you have the audacity to think Christianity is true and other religions are false, you're considered intolerant. Or a bigot. Or narrow-minded.

This is nothing more than name-calling. In logical terms, this is known as an *ad hominem* fallacy, where the person is attacked rather than the argument. If someone calls you intolerant for making a religious-truth claim, simply respond with a nondefensive question: "What do you mean by that?"

In contemporary culture, to be intolerant means you think you're right and other people are wrong. However, such a view is self-contradictory. If someone thinks we're wrong to claim that Christianity is true, then they think they are right, and we are wrong. According to their definition, they would be intolerant too!

As Christians, we need to be ready to make a case for the Christian worldview while recognizing the inherent dignity of people who hold differing opinions. It's possible to treat one another with respect even while disagreeing.

The Christian Vision of Religions and Truth

The God of the Bible is real and true. He spoke everything into existence (Ps. 33:6). After the fall of humanity, God Himself did for us what we couldn't do for ourselves: He sent His Son, Jesus. "[Jesus] himself bore our sins in his body on the tree, that we might die to sin and live to righteousness. By his wounds you have been healed" (1 Pet. 2:24).

Within this historically verifiable Story, Jesus boldly declared, "I am the way, and the truth, and the life. No one comes to the Father except through me" (John 14:6). And His closest followers, from the very beginning, repeated His exclusivist message: "There is salvation in no one else, for there is no other name under heaven given among men by which we must be saved" (Acts 4:12).

Why is Jesus the exclusive means of salvation? Because of the fall. Sin separated us from a holy God. Divine justice required punishment. Jesus is the only way because He is the only one who solved the problem of sin. No other religious leader did, or could do, what Jesus, the sinless lamb of God, did. He paid the penalty for sin and satisfied God's justice. That is why Jesus could say, "Unless you believe that I am he you will die in your sins" (John 8:24).

Rather than reject God's exclusive plan, we should be grateful in the way a diseased patient rejoices when a cure is found. The redemption and restoration we have through the exclusive means of Jesus' death and resurrection are cause for celebration. That's why it's called the gospel—it's good news. And it's available to everyone.

Navigating Pluralism

1. Know that Christianity is objectively true. God isn't real simply because we feel Him. He is real even if we *don't* feel Him. The Christian faith is based on truth. That's why apologetics—defending the Christian faith and providing reasons and evidence for its truthfulness—is essential. In order to make the case that Christianity is true, here are four questions you should be able to answer:

1. Does truth exist, and can we know it?
2. Does God exist, and what's the evidence?

3. Did Jesus rise from the dead, and what's the evidence?

4. Is the Bible trustworthy, and what's the evidence?

Thankfully, there are a multitude of Christian apologetics and world-view books, websites, curriculums, and conferences available to help answer these questions. Start with the daily BreakPoint commentaries from the Colson Center (www.breakpoint.org). Read a good apologetics book like *I Don't Have Enough Faith to Be an Atheist* by Norman Geisler and Frank Turek. Or consider attending a student conference with Impact 360 (www.impact360institute.org) or Summit Ministries (www.summit.org) to build your understanding of the truth of Christianity's claims.

2. Understand other religious views. Isolating yourself from false ideas isn't a good strategy. Eventually, you'll come face to face with other world-views through Muslim classmates, atheist professors, and Mormon friends. To be effective ambassadors for Christ in this pluralistic world, you need to be equipped to examine and challenge those worldviews.

Talk with your parents or a youth pastor about ways to interact with people of different worldviews in real life. Your family could invite Mormon neighbors for dinner. You could visit a local religious site, like a mosque or temple. Dialogue with a representative. Be friendly and ask lots of questions about what this person believes and why he or she believes it. After any of these experiences, debrief with your parents and do some research to answer any questions that come up. And always pray for the people you encounter from different religious backgrounds.

3. Ask good questions. Christians aren't the only ones who need to give reasons for what they believe. Every worldview should be able to provide evidence for its claims. When you're talking to someone with different beliefs, ask these two questions over and over again: (1) What do you mean by that? and (2) How do you know that's true?

When you ask good questions, you'll discover that many people won't know how to explain what they believe about spiritual matters or why they believe it. And that could open the door for you to share why Jesus is the way, the truth, and the life.

4. Model truth and grace in every conversation. Your goal in conversations with non-Christians is not to win an argument but to win the person. If you aren't kind and gracious, you'll be dismissed as an arrogant jerk. But if you don't have some knowledge of the truth either, you'll be dismissed as ignorant and uneducated. Like Jesus, bring truth and grace together (John 1:14).

5. Prepare for pushback. Proclaiming Jesus as the exclusive path to God won't win any popularity contests. The world is going to take offense. Think about how the apostles were treated when they proclaimed Jesus in first-century Palestine. They were arrested, brought before the authorities, ordered to stop preaching the good news, and then beaten before they were released. Their response? "They left the presence of the council, rejoicing that they were counted worthy to suffer dishonor for the name. And every day, in the temple and from house to house, they did not cease teaching and preaching that the Christ is Jesus" (Acts 5:41–42). This should be your response as well.

The Right Kind of Pluralist

Getting back to Shane and Francesca. What's the difference between them and the typical Christian student whose faith gets challenged? The answer: training. Before their encounter with their skeptical friends, they spent five days learning worldview and apologetics at a student conference. Shane and Francesca were prepared to engage the culture.

Before the camp, Francesca admitted her heart had been won by Christ through the amazing experiences she had at church, but Christianity never made sense in her mind. After taking the time to study, learn, and wrestle with opposing views, she understood that Christianity is also true rationally. In other words, her head and heart were brought together.

Shane was stronger in his faith too. Even in the face of his friends' serious objections, he had the confidence to stand up for and share God's truth.

When you go beyond "the Bible tells me so" answers and equip yourself with the rational arguments and historical evidence for God, Jesus, and Scripture, you'll also have the courage and confidence for every encounter.

Chapter Eighteen

Taking the Gospel to the Culture

"The Gospel is like a caged lion. It does not need to be
defended; it simply needs to be let out of its cage."

Charles Spurgeon, sermon (paraphrased)

Much of this book has been about defense. Indeed, the goal of this book is to help you successfully navigate the culture without drowning in it. But surviving the cultural moment isn't what we're primarily called to do. We're called to be faithful ambassadors to the culture.

In Jeremiah 28, God told Jeremiah to oppose the false prophet Hananiah, who was misleading the people of Israel regarding their time of exile in Babylon. In a very public display, Hananiah proclaimed that within two years, God would defeat the Babylonians and bring His people back to Jerusalem. He was wrong.

God wanted His people to live fully in the midst of their exile rather than withdraw and wait for rescue. Through Jeremiah, God instructed His people:

> Build houses and live in them; plant gardens and eat their produce. Take wives and have sons and daughters; take wives for your sons, and give your daughters in marriage, that they may bear sons and daughters; multiply there, and do not decrease. But seek the welfare of the city where I have sent you into exile, and pray to the

LORD on its behalf, for in its welfare you will find your
welfare. (Jer. 29:5–7)

Like the exiles, we must learn to live well in this cultural moment.
To do so, we must put our hope in the biblical Story of the world, from
creation to new creation; it is our true Story, secured by the resurrection of
Jesus Christ. The following four ideas are shaped by God's Story and will
help you confront and shape the culture around you.[1]

Celebrate, protect, promote, and preserve the good. Because God
created this world, there is beauty in the darkest times. Even when lies
dominate, truth still exists. Christians should celebrate aspects of culture
that reflect God's character and nature. Use technology for good. Tell true
stories. Enjoy beautiful art.

Contribute what is missing from our culture. Christians should *create*
culture.[2] As Jeremiah told the Israelites, building houses, having babies,
growing crops, and marrying bring good even to a pagan society. In Israel's
time of exile, Daniel offered wisdom and understanding to the government.
In the past few decades, poverty around the world has been dramatically
reduced, often because Christians have been among those providing access
to resources for wealth creation. When we create a successful business
or write a beautiful song, not only do we bring the truth, goodness, and
beauty of God into the lives of others, we also point them to the source of
those things, God Himself.

Stop the evil that we can. At times Christians must confront culture. God
hates evil. As His people, we can do no less. Throughout history, from
the British abolitionist William Wilberforce to modern-day pro-lifers,
Christians have honored God by opposing evil.

But I'm no William Wilberforce, you may think. *What influence do I
have? I don't have the platform or abilities that famous Christian activists had.*

Perhaps, but you do have the power to stop porn from infiltrating your smartphone. You can share your views about the slaughter of the innocent. You can confront the racism in your own heart. Whatever evil you can stop, you should.

Restore brokenness where we can. Many aspects of our culture are redeemable. Whenever possible, Christians should co-opt and correct culture, redirecting it to its God-given potential. Broken relationships can be reconciled. Family can be brought back together.

In these four areas we see five legitimate ways Christians can deal with the ideas, institutions, trends, fashions, and habits of our culture: *celebrate, create, confront, co-opt,* or *correct.* Beautiful art, brilliant ideas, and compelling stories should be celebrated. New, clever inventions should be created to solve contemporary problems. Lies, slander, and false religions should be confronted. New technologies can be co-opted for kingdom use. False information and misperceptions about others should be corrected and replaced with truth.

Discerning which approach is best for specific situations isn't always easy, but Christians should never be passive consumers of culture. Instead, we need to sharpen one another in the body of Christ so we can make wise decisions.

Aim for the Middle

Some Christian students mistakenly think that change will come only when they get older and acquire the controls of cultural power. God has called some of His people to high places, but He's called all of us to be faithful right in our own spheres of influence.

God has gifted you with abilities, experiences, and relationships. He has placed you in the world as His ambassadors. It is at this intersection, suggests Frederick Buechner, that you find your calling:

There are all different kinds of voices calling you to all different kinds of work, and the problem is to find out which is the voice of God.... By and large a good rule for finding out is this. The kind of work God usually calls you to is the kind of work (a) *that you need most to do* and (b) *that the world most needs to have done.*

If you really get a kick out of your work, you've presumably met requirement (a), but if your work is writing TV deodorant commercials, the chances are you've missed requirement (b). On the other hand, if your work is being a doctor in a leper colony, you have probably met requirement (b), but if most of the time you're bored or depressed by it, the chances are you have not only bypassed (a), but probably aren't helping your patients much either....

The place God calls you to is the place where your deep gladness and the world's deep hunger meet.[3]

Amen.

Notes

Chapter 1: What Culture Is and How It Shapes Us

1. Attributed to C. S. Lewis in Brian Godawa, "Postmodern Movies: The Good, the Bad, and the Relative, Part 1," *Spiritual Counterfeits Project Newsletter* 23, no. 3 (Spring 1999), www.scp-inc.org/publications/newsletters/N2303 /index.php.

2. For this section, we rely heavily on Kevin J. Vanhoozer, Charles A. Anderson, and Michael J. Sleasman, eds., "Introduction: Toward a Theory of Cultural Interpretation," in *Everyday Theology: How to Read Cultural Texts and Interpret Trends* (Grand Rapids, MI: Baker, 2007), 15–60.

3. Andy Crouch, *Culture Making: Recovering Our Creative Calling* (Downers Grove, IL: InterVarsity Books, 2008), 37.

Chapter 2: Don't Confuse the Moment and the Story

1. Rodney Stark, *The Rise of Christianity: How the Obscure, Marginal Jesus Movement Became the Dominant Religious Force in the Western World in a Few Centuries* (San Francisco: HarperSanFrancisco, 1997), chap. 5.

2. See, for example, the stories Warren Cole Smith and John Stonestreet tell in *Restoring All Things: God's Audacious Plan to Change the World through Everyday People* (Grand Rapids, MI: Baker, 2015).

3. Lesslie Newbigin, *A Walk through the Bible*, 2nd ed. (Louisville, KY: Westminster John Knox, 1999), 4.

4. For a thorough discussion of the four-chapter summary of Scripture, see Cornelius Plantinga Jr., *Engaging God's World: A Christian Vision of Faith, Learning, and Living* (Grand Rapids, MI: Eerdmans, 2002). See also Charles W. Colson and Nancy Pearcey, *How Now Shall We Live?* (Wheaton, IL: Tyndale, 1999).

Chapter 3: A Vision of Success

1. Sophie Scholl, quoted in Steven Garber, *The Fabric of Faithfulness: Weaving Together Belief and Behavior*, rev. ed. (Downers Grove, IL: InterVarsity, 2007), 188.

2. Steven Garber uses the phrase "I am Christian and I am German, therefore I am responsible for Germany" to describe the Scholls' approach to culture, but we think it also reflects Bonhoeffer's approach. See Garber, *Fabric of Faithfulness*, 180.

3. Garber, *Fabric of Faithfulness*, 176.

4. *Dietrich Bonhoeffer: Witness to Jesus Christ*, ed. John de Gruchy (Minneapolis: Augsburg Fortress, 1991), 293–94.

5. The Epicureans believed the gods were remote and detached and had lost interest in humanity. They could, therefore, live however they pleased. Unsurprisingly, Epicureanism often took the form of hedonism. The Stoics, on the other hand, were fatalists. They believed the gods determined just about every detail of human life. The apostle Paul confronted both worldviews in the Mars Hill sermon.

Chapter 4: The Information Age

1. Wikipedia, s.v. "Information Age," https://en.wikipedia.org/wiki /Information_Age.

2. Team Gwava, "How Much Data Is Created on the Internet Each Day?," *Gwava* (blog), September 8, 2016, www.gwava.com/blog/internet-data-created-daily.

3. T. S. Eliot, *The Rock: A Pageant Play* (New York: Harcourt, Brace, 1934), pt. 1, lines 15–16.

4. Neil Postman, *Amusing Ourselves to Death: Public Discourse in the Age of Show Business* (New York: Penguin, 1985).

5. Email to John Stonestreet, cited in Chuck Colson, "Can't Turn This Worldview Thing Off: Send Your Kid to Summit," *BreakPoint Commentaries*, April 6, 2015, www.breakpoint.org/bpcommentaries/entry/13/27139.

Chapter 5: The Loss of Identity

1. Chris Broussard, *Outside the Lines*, ESPN, April 29, 2013; see Chris Greenberg, "Chris Broussard, ESPN Reporter, Calls Being Gay an 'Open Rebellion to

God,'" *Huffington Post*, April 30, 2013, www.huffingtonpost.com/2013 /04/29/chris-broussard-espn-nba-gay-reaction_n_3180080.html.

2. Luc Ferry, *Learning to Live: A Young Person's Guide*, trans. Theo Cuffe (Edinburgh, Scotland: Canongate Books, 2006), 72.

3. Blaise Pascal, *Pensées*, trans. A. J. Krailsheimer (New York: Penguin, 1995), 45.

4. For a helpful description of the postmodern worldview, see W. Gary Phillips, William E. Brown, and John Stonestreet, *Making Sense of Your World: A Biblical Worldview*, 2nd ed. (Salem, WI: Sheffield, 2008), 48–58.

5. James E. Marcia et al., *Ego Identity: A Handbook for Psychosocial Research* (New York: Springer, 1993). For a helpful summary, see "Marcia's States of Adolescent Identity Development," YouTube video, posted by Tiffany Dickie, January 31, 2014, www.youtube.com/watch?v=a8HIY_bqrVo. Only a portion of Marcia's theory is discussed here. We're indebted to Dr. Peter Cha, my (John's) seminary professor at Trinity International University, who first pointed me to Marcia's theory and applied it to the context of the church and home.

6. This is our paraphrase of Steven Garber, who rightly points out that for a world-view to last, it must be "sufficient for the questions and crises …, particularly the challenge of modern and postmodern consciousness with its implicit secularization and pluralization." See Steven Garber, *Fabric of Faithfulness*, 51, 122–32.

Chapter 6: Being Alone Together

1. Sherry Turkle, *Alone Together: Why We Expect More from Technology and Less from Each Other* (New York: Basic Books, 2011). Her February 2012 TED talk "Connected, but Alone?" offers a helpful summary of the book, as well as many of the points we discuss in this chapter. See www.ted.com/talks /sherry_turkle_alone_together?language=en.

2. Glenn Enoch et al., *The Nielson Total Audience Report: Q1 2016* (New York: Nielson, 2016), 4, cited in Jacqueline Howard, "Americans Devote More Than 10 Hours a Day to Screen Time, and Growing," CNN, July 29, 2016, www.cnn.com/2016/06/30/health/americans-screen-time-nielsen/.

3. We're grateful to John's colleague Shane Morris for articulating these consequences in this very helpful format. Shane has been thinking and writing about technology for some time, and these thoughts were communicated to John in an email, October 5, 2016.

4. For a full description of each of these lies, and to read the single best book available for parents on helping kids navigate the digital age, see Kathy Koch, *Screens and Teens: Connecting with Our Kids in a Wireless World* (Chicago: Moody, 2015).

5. See Centers for Disease Control and Prevention, "Suicide Trends among Persons Aged 10–24 Years—United States 1994–2012," *Morbidity and Mortality Weekly Report* 64, no. 8 (March 2015): 201–5, www.cdc.gov/mmwr/preview /mmwrhtml/mm6408a1.htm.

6. Research cited in Anne Fishel, "The Most Important Thing You Can Do with Your Kids? Eat Dinner with Them," *Washington Post*, January 12, 2015, www.washingtonpost.com/posteverything/wp/2015/01/12/the-most-important-thing-you-can-do-with-your-kids-eat-dinner-with-them/?utm_term =.b61005c506d0.

7. Jean Twenge, "Teens Are Sleeping Less—but There's a Surprisingly Easy Fix," The Conversation, October 19, 2017, https://theconversation.com/ teens-are-sleeping-less-but-theres-a-surprisingly-easy-fix-85157.

Chapter 7: Pornography

1. Barna Group, *The Porn Phenomenon: The Explosive Growth of Pornography and How It's Impacting Your Church, Life, and Ministry* (Ventura, CA: Barna Group, 2016), cited in Chrissy Gordon, "Josh McDowell Ministry and Barna Group Unveil Key Findings for *The Porn Phenomenon*," Josh McDowell Ministry, January 19, 2016, www.josh.org/news-release/key-findings -for-the-porn-phenomenon-unveiled/.

2. Josh McDowell Ministry, *The Porn Phenomenon: The Impact of Pornography in the Digital Age* (Ventura, CA: Barna Group, 2016).

3. Josh McDowell Ministry, *Porn Phenomenon*.

4. Data from multiple sources cited in Covenant Eyes, "Pornography Statistics: Annual Report 2015," www.covenanteyes.com/pornstats/. For full report with original sources, download the report from the website: Covenant Eyes, *Pornography Statistics: 250+ Facts, Quotes, and Statistics about Pornography Use* (Owosso, MI: Covenant Eyes, 2015).

5. Joe S. McIlhaney Jr. and Freda McKissic Bush, *Hooked: New Science on How Casual Sex Is Affecting Our Children* (Chicago: Northfield Publishing, 2008).

6. Fight the New Drug, *Harmful Effects of Pornography: 2016 Reference Guide* (San Francisco: Fight the New Drug, 2016), http://store.fightthenewdrug.org

/collections/books/products/harmful-effects-of-pornography-2016
-reference-guide.

7. Judith Reisman, et al., "Hearing on the Brain Science behind Pornography
   Addiction and the Effects of Addiction on Families and Communities,"
   Hearing to US Senate Committee on Commerce, Science, and Transportation,
   November 18, 2004, www.hudsonbyblow.com/wp
   -content/uploads/2018/01/2004SenateTestimony.pdf.

8. "Hilton Announces Removal of All Porn Channels from Hotels," LifeSiteNews.
   com, August 20, 2015, www.lifesitenews.com/news/public-blitz-forces
   -hilton-hotels-to-drop-porn.

9. "Russell Brand Talks Sex, Softcore & Hardcore Porn," YouTube video, posted by
   Fight the New Drug, February 23, 2015, www.youtube.com/watch?v
   =5kvzamjQW9M.

10. Terry Crews's Facebook page, accessed December 30, 2016, www.facebook
    .com/realterrycrews/videos/1083942814959410/.

11. Shmuley Boteach and Pamela Anderson, "Take the Pledge: No More Indulging
    Porn," *Wall Street Journal*, August 31, 2016, www.wsj.com/articles/take-the
    -pledge-no-more-indulging-porn-1472684658.

Chapter 8: The Hookup Culture

1. Sade Patterson, "Campus Sex Week: Abortion Is Healthy, Bible Supports
   Homosexual Sex, Orgies Are Fun," College Fix, November 24, 2015,
   www.thecollegefix.com/post/25234/.

2. Sade Patterson, "This College Student Taught Campus Feminists What a Real 'Sex
   Week' Looks Like," College Fix, April 5, 2016, www.thecollegefix.com
   /post/26884/.

3. Jean M. Twenge, Ryne A. Sherman, and Brooke E. Wells, "Sexual Inactivity during Young Adulthood Is More Common among U.S. Millennials and iGen:
   Age, Period, and Cohort Effects on Having No Sexual Partners after Age 18,"
   Archives of Sexual Behavior (August 2016): 1–8, http://link.springer
   .com/article/10.1007/s10508-016-0798-z.

4. Centers for Disease Control and Prevention, "Youth Risk Behavior Surveillance—
   United States, 2015," *Morbidity and Mortality Weekly Report (MMWR)* 65, no. 6
   (June 2016): 27, www.cdc.gov/healthyyouth/data/yrbs
   /pdf/2015/ss6506_updated.pdf.

5. Centers for Disease Control and Prevention, "Sexually Transmitted Disease Surveillance, 2014," cited in Centers for Disease Control and Prevention, "CDC Fact Sheet: Reported STDs in the United States; 2014 National Data for Chlamydia, Gonorrhea, and Syphilis," November 2015, www.cdc.gov /std/stats14/std-trends-508.pdf.

6. Centers for Disease Control and Prevention, "CDC Fact Sheet: Incidence, Prevalence, and Cost of Sexually Transmitted Infections in the United States," February 2013, www.cdc.gov/std/stats/sti-estimates-fact-sheet-feb-2013.pdf.

7. Robyn L. Fielder et al., "Sexual Hookups and Adverse Health Outcomes: A Longitudinal Study of First-Year College Women," *Journal of Sex Research* 51, no. 2 (2014): 131–44, www.ncbi.nlm.nih.gov/pmc/articles/PMC3946692/.

8. Sara E. Sandberg-Thoma and Claire M. Kamp Dush, "Casual Sexual Relationships and Mental Health in Adolescence and Emerging Adulthood," *Journal of Sex Research* 51, no. 2 (2014): 121–30, www.tandfonline.com/doi /abs/10.1080/00224499.2013.821440.

9. Jennifer L. Walsh et al., "Do Alcohol and Marijuana Use Decrease the Probability of Condom Use for College Women?," *Journal of Sex Research* 51, no. 2 (2014): 145–58, www.tandfonline.com/doi/abs/10.1080/00224499 .2013.821442.

10. Kay Hymowitz et al., *Knot Yet: The Benefits and Costs of Delayed Marriage in America* (Charlottesville, VA: National Marriage Project, 2013), 14, http://nationalmarriageproject.org/wp-content/uploads/2013/03/KnotYet-FinalForWeb.pdf.

11. Galena K. Rhoades and Scott M. Stanley, *Before "I Do": What Do Premarital Experiences Have to Do with Marital Quality among Today's Young Adults?* (Charlottesville, VA: National Marriage Project, 2014), 5, http://nationalmarriageproject.org/wordpress/wp-content/ uploads/2014/08/NMP-BeforeIDoReport-Final.pdf.

Chapter 9: Sexual Orientation

1. See Rosaria Champagne Butterfield, *The Secret Thoughts of an Unlikely Convert: An English Professor's Journey into Christian Faith*, rev. ed. (Pittsburgh: Covenant and Crown, 2014).

2. Lawrence S. Mayer and Paul R. McHugh, "Sexuality and Gender: Findings from the Biological, Psychological, and Social Sciences," *New Atlantis*, no. 50 (Fall 2016): 14, 31, www.thenewatlantis.com/docLib/20160819 _TNA50SexualityandGender.pdf.

3. For example, see J. Michael Bailey et al., "Genetic and Environmental Influences on Sexual Orientation and Its Correlates in an Australian Twin Sample," *Journal of Personality and Social Psychology* 78, no. 3 (March 2000): 524–36, www.ncbi.nlm.nih.gov/pubmed/10743878.

4. "What Causes a Person to Have a Particular Sexual Orientation?" in American Psychological Association, "Sexual Orientation and Homosexuality: Answers to Your Questions for a Better Understanding," accessed October 4, 2016, www.apa.org/topics/lgbt/orientation.aspx.

5. See Stanton L. Jones and Mark A. Yarhouse, *Ex-Gays? A Longitudinal Study of Religiously Mediated Change in Sexual Orientation* (Downers Grove, IL: InterVarsity, 2007).

6. Peter Sprigg and Timothy Dailey, eds., "What Causes Homosexuality?," chap. 1 in *Getting It Straight: What the Research Shows about Homosexuality* (Washington, DC: Family Research Council, 2004), http://downloads.frc .org/EF/EF08L41.pdf.

7. Edward O. Laumann et al., *The Social Organization of Sexuality: Sexual Practices in the United States* (Chicago: University of Chicago Press, 1994), 216.

8. James H. Price et al., "Perceptions of Cervical Cancer and Pap Smear Screening Behavior by Women's Sexual Orientation," *Journal of Community Health* 21, no. 2 (April 1996): 89–105; Daron G. Ferris et al., "A Neglected Lesbian Health Concern: Cervical Neoplasia," *Journal of Family Practice* 43, no. 6 (December 1996): 581; C. J. Skinner et al., "A Case-Controlled Study of the Sexual Health Needs of Lesbians," *Genitourinary Medicine* 72, no. 4 (August 1996): 277–80.

9. Centers for Disease Control and Prevention, "Sexually Transmitted Disease Surveillance, 2014," cited in Centers for Disease Control and Prevention, "CDC Fact Sheet: Reported STDs in the United States; 2014 National Data for Chlamydia, Gonorrhea, and Syphilis," November 2015, www.cdc.gov /std/stats14/std-trends-508.pdf.

10. Centers for Disease Control and Prevention, "HIV among Gay and Bisexual Men: Fast Facts," September 30, 2016, www.cdc.gov/hiv/group/msm/index. html.

11. Centers for Disease Control and Prevention, "Sexual Identity, Sex of Sexual Contacts, and Health-Related Behaviors among Students in Grades 9–12— United States and Selected Sites, 2015," *Morbidity and Mortality Weekly Report (MMWR) Surveillance Summaries* 65, no. 9 (August 2016): 1–202, www.cdc.gov/mmwr/volumes/65/ss/ss6509a1.htm.

12. For the Netherlands, see Theo G. M. Sandfort et al., "Same-Sex Sexual Behavior and Psychiatric Disorders: Findings from the Netherlands Mental Health Survey and Incidence Study (NEMESIS)," *Archives of General Psychiatry* 58, no. 1 (January 2001): 88–89. For England, see Apu Chakraborty et al., "Mental Health of the Non-heterosexual Population of England," *British Journal of Psychiatry* 198, no. 2 (February 2011): 143–48. For New Zealand, see David M. Fergusson, L. John Horwood, and Annette L. Beautrais, "Is Sexual Orientation Related to Mental Health Problems and Suicidality in Young People?," *Archives of General Psychiatry* 56, no. 10 (October 1999): 876–80.

13. Leslie Walker, "How to Edit Gender Identity Status on Facebook," Lifewire, June 24, 2019, www.lifewire.com/edit-gender-identity-status-on -facebook-2654421.

14. See Christopher Yuan and Angela Yuan, *Out of a Far Country: A Gay Son's Journey to God; A Broken Mother's Search for Hope* (Colorado Springs: WaterBrook, 2011).

Chapter 10: Gender Identity

1. Wikipedia, s.v. "Cisgender," https://en.wikipedia.org/wiki/Cisgender.

2. "College Kids Say the Darndest Things: On Identity," video produced by Family Policy Institute of Washington, April 13, 2016, www.youtube.com /watch?v=xfO1veFs6Ho.

3. Susan Donaldson James, "Pittsburgh Man Thinks He's a Dog, Goes by Name 'Boomer,'" ABC News, November 6, 2013, http://abcnews.go.com/Health /pittsburgh-man-thinks-dog-boomer/story?id=20801512.

4. Candace Amos, "Transgender Woman Leaves Wife and 7 Kids to Live as a 6-Year-Old Girl," *New York Daily News*, December 12, 2015, accessed October 16, 2016, www.nydailynews.com/news/world/ transgender-woman-leaves-wife-7-kids-live-girl-article-1.2463795.

5. Carolyn Moynihan, "Alas, Marrying Oneself Is Now a Thing … Really," *Stream*, September 3, 2016, https://stream.org/marrying-oneself-now-a-thing/.

6. Bradford Richardson, "New York Businesses Face Hefty Penalties for 'Misgendering' Customers," *Washington Times*, May 18, 2016, www.washingtontimes.com/news/2016/may/18/de-blasio-fine -businesses-wrong-gender-pronouns/.

7. Stella Morabito, "Trouble in Transtopia: Murmurs of Sex Change Regret," *Federalist*, November 11, 2014, http://thefederalist.com/2014/11/11 /trouble-in-transtopia-murmurs-of-sex-change-regret/.

8. You can find many of his articles at the following websites: (1) *Federalist*— http://thefederalist.com/author/walt-heyer/; and (2) *Public Discourse*— www.thepublicdiscourse.com/author/walt-heyer/.

9. Paul McHugh, "Transgenderism: A Pathogenic Meme," *Public Discourse*, June 10, 2015, www.thepublicdiscourse.com/2015/06/15145/.

Chapter 11: Affluence and Consumerism

1. Barna Group and Impact 360 Institute, *Gen Z: The Culture, Beliefs and Motivations Shaping the Next Generation* (2018): 38, 40.

2. *Gen Z*, 38.

3. *Gen Z*, 40.

4. Laura A. Pratt, Debra J. Brody, and Quiping Gu, "Antidepressant Use in Persons Aged 12 and Over: United States, 2005–2008," *NCHS Data Brief*, no. 76 (October 2011): 1, www.cdc.gov/nchs/data/databriefs/db76.htm.

5. Jean M. Twenge et al., "Birth Cohort Increases in Psychopathology among Young Americans, 1938–2007: A Cross-Temporal Meta-analysis of the MMPI," *Clinical Psychology Review* 30, no. 2 (March 2010): 145–54, www.ncbi.nlm.nih.gov/pubmed/19945203.

6. S. S. Luthar and C. Sexton, "The High Price of Affluence," in R. Kail, ed., *Advances in Child Development* (San Diego: Academic Press, 2005); and M. Csikszentmihalyi and B. Schneider, *Becoming Adult: How Teenagers Prepare for the World of Work* (New York: Basic Books, 2000), cited in Madeline Levine, *The Price of Privilege: How Parental Pressure and Material Advantage Are Creating a Generation of Disconnected and Unhappy Kids* (New York: HarperCollins, 2008), 17.

7. Charles H. Spurgeon, *Evening by Evening: A New Edition of the Classic Devotional Based on the Holy Bible, English Standard Version*, ed. Alistair Begg (Wheaton, IL: Crossway, 2007), 339.

8. Derrick Feldmann et al., *Cause, Influence, and the Next Generation: The 2015 Millennial Impact Workforce Report* (West Palm Beach, FL: Achieve/Millennial Impact Project, 2015), http://fi.fudwaca.com/mi/files/2015/07/2015 -MillennialImpactReport.pdf.

Chapter 12: Addiction

1. Maggie Fox, "Americans Are Drinking More—a Lot More," NBC News, April 23, 2015, www.nbcnews.com/health/health-news/americans-are-drinking -more-lot-more-n347126.

2. Caleb Diehl and Michael Schramm, "Study: Daily Marijuana Use among College Students at Highest Rate in 35 Years," *USA Today College*, September 1, 2015, http://college.usatoday.com/2015/09/01/study-daily-marijuana-use -among-college-students-at-highest-rate-in-35-years/.

3. "Heroin: The Poisoning of America," CNN, October 17, 2016, www.cnn.com/2016/10/13/health/heroin-poisoning-of-america/.

4. E. J. Mundell, "US Opioid Crisis Is Top Health Story of 2018," WebMD, December 27, 2018, www.webmd.com/mental-health/addiction/news /20181227/us-opioid-crisis-is-top-health-story-of-2018#1.

5. National Institute on Drug Abuse, "Monitoring the Future Survey, Overview of Findings 2015," revised December 2015, www.drugabuse.gov/related-topics /trends-statistics/monitoring-future/monitoring-future-survey-overview -findings-2015.

6. Research cited in National Institute on Alcohol Abuse and Alcoholism, "College Drinking," December 2015, http://pubs.niaaa.nih.gov/publications /CollegeFactSheet/CollegeFactSheet.pdf.

7. Sushrut Jangi, "Can We Please Stop Pretending Marijuana Is Harmless?," *Boston Globe*, October 8, 2015, www.bostonglobe.com/magazine/2015/10/08/can -please-stop-pretending-marijuana-harmless/MneQebFPWg79ifTAXc1PkM /story.html. See also National Institute on Drug Abuse, "Want to Know More? Some FAQs about Marijuana," "Marijuana: Facts for Teens," May 2015, www.drugabuse.gov/publications/marijuana-facts-teens/want-to -know-more-some-faqs-about-marijuana.

8. Jennifer Alsever, "Is Pot Losing Its Buzz in Colorado?," *Fortune*, June 29, 2016, http://fortune.com/pot-marijuana-colorado/.

9. Wayne Drash and Max Blau, "In America's Drug Death Capital: How Heroin Is Scarring the Next Generation," CNN, September 16, 2016, www.cnn.com /2016/09/16/health/huntington-heroin/index.html. See also Corky Siemaszko, "Ohio City Releases Shocking Photos to Show Effects of 'Poison Known as Heroin,'" NBC News, September 10, 2016, www.nbcnews.com/news/us -news/ohio-city-releases-shocking-photo-show-effects-poison-known -heroin-n645806.

10. What about medicinal marijuana? We should distinguish the intent to get high (recreational marijuana) from the intent to heal (medical marijuana). A systematic review of the scientific research is inconclusive about the medical benefits. Research should continue before we start enacting public policy. See Penny F. Whiting et al., "Cannabinoids for Medical Use: A Systematic Review and Meta-analysis," *JAMA* 313, no. 24 (June 2015): 2456–73, http://jamanetwork.com/journals/jama/fullarticle/2338251.

11. National Center on Addiction and Substance Abuse at Columbia University, "The Importance of Family Dinners VIII," September 2012, www.centeronaddiction.org/addiction-research/reports/importance-of-family-dinners-2012.

12. "Brian Welch—White Chair Film—I Am Second," YouTube video, published November 20, 2012, www.youtube.com/watch?v=q6EIhkAyy3s.

Chapter 13: Entertainment

1. George Lucas, interview by Bill Moyers, in "Of Myth and Men," *Time*, April 18, 1999, http://content.time.com/time/magazine/article/0,9171,23298-3,00.html.

2. Bruno Mars and Cardi B, "Please Me," Sony/ATV Music Publishing LLC, 2019.

3. Courtney Love, interview by Philip Weiss, in "The Love Issue," *Spin*, October 1998, 100.

4. John M. Culkin, "A Schoolman's Guide to Marshall McLuhan," *Saturday Review*, March 18, 1967, 51–53.

5. Kirsten Corder et al., "Revising on the Run or Studying on the Sofa: Prospective Associations between Physical Activity, Sedentary Behaviour, and Exam Results in British Adolescents," *International Journal of Behavioral Nutrition and Physical Activity* 12, no. 106 (September 2015), http://ijbnpa.biomedcentral.com/articles/10.1186/s12966-015-0269-2.

6. Emma Green, "Lecrae: 'Christians Have Prostituted Art to Give Answers,'" *Atlantic*, October 6, 2014, www.theatlantic.com/entertainment/archive/2014/10/lecrae-christians-have-prostituted-art-to-give-answers/381103/.

Chapter 14: Racial Tension

1. Natalie Angier, "Do Races Differ? Not Really, Genes Show," *New York Times*, August 22, 2000, www.nytimes.com/2000/08/22/science/do-races-differ-not-really-genes-show.html.

2. Wesley Lowery and Kimberly Kindy, "These Are the Racially Charged E-mails That Got 3 Ferguson Police and Court Officials Fired," *Washington Post*, April 3, 2015, www.washingtonpost.com/news/post-nation/wp/2015/04/03/these-are-the-racist-e-mails-that-got-3-ferguson-police-and-court-officials-fired/.

3. Eliott C. McLaughlin, "'Disgraceful' University of Oklahoma Fraternity Shuttered after Racist Chant," CNN, March 10, 2015, www.cnn.com/2015/03/09/us/oklahoma-fraternity-chant/.

4. Samuel Chamberlain, "Fox News Contributor Lawrence Jones Faces Racist Taunts from Protesters at 'Impeach Trump' Rally," Fox News, June 17, 2019, www.foxnews.com/entertainment/lawrence-jones-fox-news-racist-taunts-impeach-trump-rally.

5. Orlando Patterson, "Race, Gender, and Liberal Fallacies," Opinion, *New York Times*, October 20, 1991, www.nytimes.com/1991/10/20/opinion/op-ed-race-gender-and-liberal-fallacies.html.

6. Catie Edmondson and Jasmine C. Lee, "Meet the New Freshmen in Congress," *New York Times*, January 3, 2019, www.nytimes.com/interactive/2018/11/28/us/politics/congress-freshman-class.html.

7. Harold Dollar, *St. Luke's Missiology: A Cross-Cultural Challenge* (Pasadena, CA: William Carey Library, 1996), 22.

8. Frank Newport, "Americans Today Much More Accepting of a Woman, Black, Catholic, or Jew as President," Gallup, March 29, 1999, www.gallup.com/poll/3979/americans-today-much-more-accepting-woman-black-catholic.aspx.

Chapter 15: How to Read the Bible

1. "State of the Bible 2018: Seven Top Findings," Barna Group, July 10, 2018, www.barna.com/research/state-of-the-bible-2018-seven-top-findings/.

2. Barna Group and Impact 360 Institute, *Gen Z: The Culture, Beliefs and Motivations Shaping the Next Generation* (2018): 25.

Chapter 16: Why to Trust the Bible

1. William Lane Craig, "God Is Not Dead Yet: How Current Philosophers Argue for His Existence," *Christianity Today*, July 3, 2008, www.christianitytoday.com/ct/2008/july/13.22.html.

2. For an excellent video introduction to the transmission of the New Testament, watch Dr. Daniel Wallace's presentation "Did Copyists Copy the New

Testament Correctly?," YouTube video, published April 1, 2015,
www.youtube.com/watch?v=AklwfTtAFoM.

3. For an excellent introduction to the reliability of the New Testament, read
    J. Warner Wallace's book *Cold-Case Christianity: A Homicide Detective
    Investigates the Claims of the Gospels* (Colorado Springs: David C Cook, 2013).

Chapter 18: Taking the Gospel to the Culture

1. See Warren Cole Smith and John Stonestreet, *Restoring All Things: God's Audacious
    Plan to Change the World through Everyday People* (Grand Rapids, MI: Baker,
    2015), 25–26. See also David Kinnaman and Gabe Lyons, *Good Faith: Being a
    Christian When Society Thinks You're Irrelevant and Extreme* (Grand Rapids, MI:
    Baker, 2016), 79–91.

2. See Andy Crouch, *Culture Making: Recovering Our Creative Calling* (Downers
    Grove, IL: InterVarsity, 2013).

3. Frederick Buechner, "Vocation," in *Wishful Thinking: A Theological ABC* (New
    York: Harper and Row, 1973), 95. For a thorough description of the idea of
    calling, see Smith and Stonestreet, "Conclusion: Two Personal Stories," in
    Restoring All Things, 203–8.